PREVIOUS
CONVICTIONS

PREVIOUS

CONVICTIONS

Conversion in the Real World
Edited by Martyn Percy

SPCK

Published in Great Britain in 2000 by
Society for Promoting Christian Knowledge
Holy Trinity Church
Marylebone Road
London NW1 4DU

British Library Cataloguing-in-Publication Data

A catalogue record for this book is available from the British Library

ISBN 0–281–05180–1

Typeset by Wilmaset Ltd, Birkenhead, Wirral
Printed in Great Britain by
Arrowsmiths, Bristol

CONTENTS

CONTRIBUTORS

Canon Dr Martyn Percy is Director of the Lincoln Theological Institute, University of Sheffield.

Dr Sara Savage teaches the Psychology of Religion in the Cambridge Federation of Theological Colleges, and is part of the Centre for Advanced Religious and Theological Studies, University of Cambridge.

The Rt Revd Hugh Montefiore lives in London, and is the former Bishop of Birmingham.

Revd Dr Anne Townsend is an Anglican priest, author and counsellor, based in London.

Professor Eileen Barker is Professor of Sociology, London School of Economics, and Director of INFORM.

Professor Paul Heelas is Professor of Religious Studies, Lancaster University.

Dr Paul Freston lectures in Religious Studies in the University of Oxford and in South America.

Tim Winter teaches Islamic Studies at the University of Cambridge.

Canon Dr Andrew Wingate is Principal of the College of the Ascension, Birmingham.

Canon Timothy Yates is the author of *Christian Missions in the Twentieth Century* (CUP, 1994), and a clergyman in North Derbyshire.

INTRODUCTION

Martyn Percy

Before I reached my early teens, I went forward at a Christian rally and gave my life to God. I forget the precise date and venue. But I remember it being in a marquee somewhere near Watford, a bus load of us having travelled from our local church youth group. There were hymns, a choir, a rousing sermon, and an 'altar call', in which the preacher invited any who 'had not given their life to the Lord' to get up out of their seats, come to the front, meet a counsellor, pray a prayer and receive some free literature. Of course, initially, nobody moves: this is England, after all. And the English are a quintessentially reserved people, who like being at the back of orderly queues that move rather slowly.

Eventually I did pluck up courage and go forward, with my mate Jim – I think we had figured out that we were as likely to be guilty of sin as any other folk. We prayed our prayer of commitment, received our literature, and went home on the bus rejoicing – changed people.

Changed, that is, until the next time there was a rally or crusade. Growing up evangelical, as I did, mostly, it was not unusual to give your life to Christ several times, and I was no exception to that statistic. 'Dedication', 're-dedication', 'affirmation', 'commitment', 're-commitment', 'assurance' – and in the maelstrom of teenage years, with guilt bursting into your psyche with as much frequency as the spots on your face, you could be forgiven for feeling as though you were drowning in a cauldron of your own hormones. Quite simply, you are not sure of very much in those 'wonder years'; religion for me, at least, gave me an important anchor.

I do not regret a single one of my responses to an altar call. But of course, I now see them in a different perspective. I now see that my baptism, even as an infant, was a fundamental adoption into the life of Christ – into which I slowly grew, and continue gradually to come to own. Archbishop Michael Ramsay, when once asked what was the 'best day of his life' replied that he knew what it was and when it was, but had no memory of it: it was his baptism. It was confirmation for me, at the age of 14, by Robert Runcie, that stopped me 're-committing' myself virtually every time an altar call came along. I realized that what I affirmed, God had confirmed in me: it would take a lifetime to respond. The Christian life is a marathon, not a sprint. It is not possible to hand over 'the whole of our lives' to God at once, because we live, and as we live, we change – hopefully, though, from glory to glory. To be a Christian is to be a 'becoming person'.

If becoming a Christian was complicated for me, how much more so must it have been for the first disciples – Jewish heretics with a big identity problem, with a dead leader who, they claimed, was alive; beating off wild rumours that this sect were cannibals, eating the body and blood of their founder. It is not a very promising start for a new religion.

Oddly, the New Testament offers very little help in telling us what a Christian actually is. Paul argued that Christians were 'those who had the Spirit of Christ' – a self-selecting and self-qualifying phrase. Or, they had to 'confess Jesus as Lord' – again, a very inclusive definition. What kind of 'Lord', exactly? Lord of my life, lord of the manor, lord of my sect, or lord of the universe? Paul doesn't say. His conversion was dramatic; but many are not – they are slow pilgrimages that wend their way through the highways and byways of life. To have a dramatic experience does not necessarily lead to conversion. So what does it mean to turn to Christ? With a rather Jewish spin, Luke, the writer of Acts, gives an insight into who Christians are by telling us, not what they believe – there are no creeds yet, or New Testament, or Alternative Service Book, Book of Common Prayer or Church of England – but what they *do*. Christians, we learn:

- have been baptized – probably young and old alike;
- break bread and pray – as a community;
- perform miracles and give alms.

Today, few people come to faith because they have been convinced by a powerful preacher, or by the sight of a miracle. What brings people to lasting faith is the quality of help, friendship and life offered by the Church, and the relationships made in and beyond its boundaries. This is how the resurrection is lived – by ordinary day-to-day Christian living. From this flows the 'abundant life' that Jesus speaks about – a fullness of being that makes sense of joy and suffering, bound up in Jesus' resurrected body. This is what the Church is to become: a holding together of celebration and consolation, life and death, birth and decay, pain and joy.

So what exactly is conversion? The term itself is part of everyday language, and simply means 'to turn' – one currency into another, electricity into light or heat, or ingredients into a meal. The widespread use of the word carries over into the field of religious studies and theology. A 'convert' is someone who has turned away from something and embraced a faith; but this faith need not be new, for conversion can be 're-turning'.

Studies and narratives of conversion have a long history within religions, including Christianity. Augustine's *Confessions* functions as an ideal 'template' for conversion in the ancient world as much as David Wilkerson's *The Cross and the Switchblade* has done for some in the modern world. And yet in spite of much study of the phenomena, some of which is exemplary (e.g. William James, Lewis Rambo, and others), scholars have barely scratched the surface of the subject. Theologians are often squeamish about prying too far into the realms of religious experience. Those engaged in the social scientific study of religion (e.g. sociology, anthropology, psychology, etc.) have often been guilty of reductive studies, which have done less than justice to the richness of the experiences. Correspondingly, little is really known about converts and the process of conversion.

For example, to what extent do rallies and crusades really 'work'? Is a course like Alpha mainly a 'refresher' for like-minded Christians, or something that appeals to non-religious people? Do people who join 'cults' do so freely? Is it true that Roman Catholicism is losing ground to Pentecostalism in South America? Why do people join New Religious Movements? How can you convert to Islam (using the World Wide Web)? Why do some people change from one faith to another – and at what cost?

This book is an exploration of the single yet complex issue of conversion. It uses a blend of authors from different fields in order to elucidate the subject for students of religious studies: theology and the social sciences are both taken seriously. Most of the authors in this volume delivered their papers as lectures in Sheffield Cathedral in 1998, under the auspices of the Lincoln Theological Institute for the Study of Religion and Society, which is a research institute of the University of Sheffield. The central question each lecturer addressed was this: why do people change? In the essays that follow – which range over Judaism, Islam, various types of Christianity, 'cults' and New Religious Movements – the authors set out to illuminate the study of conversion, and throw light on the key reasons for movement within a religion, movement away from one, or embracing a new faith.

This book does not wish to restrict the consideration of conversion in line with one particular, narrow definition. Instead, it sets out to

describe a variety of types of conversion and the processes that relate
to them, seeing conversion not as a singular phenomenon but as a
complex and multi-faceted form of change. Correspondingly, the
subjects and authors represent a range of perspectives and traditions. Sara Savage introduces the study of conversion from a psychological perspective. Two authors describe and reflect on conversion
from one faith to another: Hugh Montefiore on the journey from
Judaism to Christianity, and Anne Townsend, in a provocatively
titled essay ('Out of the Playpen') on the transition from evangelicalism to liberalism. Eileen Barker (London School of Economics
and INFORM) and Paul Heelas explore dimensions of conversion
in New Religious Movements (NRMs). Paul Freston and Andrew
Wingate examine how cultures in other parts of the world impact
on the study of conversion (South America and India). Two final
essays look at theories of conversion in the context of Christian missiology (Timothy Yates), and some experiences of conversion in
Islam (Tim Winter). The essays are intentionally introductory:
this is a huge field. Yet the contributions are here to serve as useful
markers that can offer a preliminary guide to the reader, introdu-
cing the vastness of the territory.

According to the American scholar Lewis Rambo, one of the best
mappers of the territory, the concept of conversion, although used
primarily in Christianity, Judaism and Islam to refer to the process
of joining a religion, is associated with various forms of personal and
communal change. Throughout religious history one can observe a
great variety of transformations of individuals and groups which
vary in intensity and duration. Nearly all religions or religious
groups have identifiable rites of passage and initiation, many of
which involve ways either of converting outsiders to 'insider' status,
or of reallocating roles to those who were once insiders but who have
lost their status or role within the group. Rambo considers that conversion should be understood as having three dimensions: tradition,
transformation and transcendence. In practice these dimensions in-
teract and are not discrete, but to distinguish between them is useful
for a better understanding of conversion.

'Tradition' refers to the historical and contextual aspects of both
the convert and the religious group, taking into account such
aspects of the conversion process as relationships with group
members and non-group members, the previous life of the convert,
the institutional aspect of the religion, its symbols, rituals and so
on, and the social situation in which conversion takes place. From
a more anthropological stance, ideological and cultural aspects of
tradition may be considered and the way in which culture impacts
on conversion and vice versa.

'Transformation' encompasses personal aspects of change in thoughts, beliefs and actions through a study of experience, selfhood and consciousness. This may be done through the discipline of psychology, an example being studies such as William James's *The Varieties of Religious Experience*, which focuses upon factors which may predispose individuals towards conversion such as anguish, conflict or guilt. Various schools of thought in psychology may focus on different aspects of the experience of conversion and interpret them in different ways; for example, psychoanalytic psychologists may focus on the relationship between the convert and his or her parents, while the behaviourist may address aspects of conditioning and behavioural reinforcement.

'Transcendence' refers to encounter with the sacred, that which is for many religions the goal of conversion. From the perspective of the theologian, the perceived relationship with the divine inherent in religious experience is central to an analysis of conversion. Again, according to Rambo, these three dimensions of conversion – tradition, transformation and transcendence – lead to at least five different types of conversion:

1 *Tradition transition* refers to conversion from one major or traditional religion to another. This may occur on a large scale through exposure to different cultures, an example of which is the expansion of conversion to Christianity in other cultures following European colonialization in the eighteenth, nineteenth and twentieth centuries.
2 *Institutional transition* involves changing allegiance from one subgroup within a major religion to another, for example switching between denominations of Christianity either for convenience of location or because of religious experience or shift in belief.
3 *Affiliation* is the process of a group or individual without previous religious commitment becoming involved with a religious community. This has been regarded as problematic in analysis because of allegations of brainwashing among New Religious Movements.
4 *Intensification* is used to refer to renewed commitment within an existing previous religious affiliation, a deepening of commitment or a making central to life that which was previously peripheral.
5 *Apostasy* refers to a rejection and defection from a previous religious group or orientation which does not involve a commitment to a new religious system but leads to the adoption of a new or prior system of non-religious beliefs or values. The processes involved in leaving a group are important in the study of personal change; in particular, study has focused on the forced

'deprogramming' and defection from New Religious Movements.

Each of these types involves a different degree of change and a different process of conversion; some require a major reconstitution of belief system and dislocation on a cultural level, whereas others only require a minimal degree of social or institutional movement. It is therefore possible, argues Rambo, to present a model of the process involved in conversion which can be broken down into a number of stages. This is not put forward as a universal, but rather as a way of organizing the diverse literature which exists on the subject. For example, the relevant contexts of conversion can be addressed, which might include the social, cultural, religious and personal circumstances of the individual. In turn, those contexts can be usefully broken down into macro- and micro-elements.

An example of macro-context might be a consideration of the social, cultural and institutional circumstances of the society in which conversion takes place. Secularization, and the pluralist culture which exists in contemporary British society, may be seen as things which promote uncertainty and the choice of a new religious orientation in order to find meaning and grounding in life. An example of a micro-context could be more concerned with the immediate interactions of the individual convert. This involves their family situation, religious life and peer group, and refers to the way in which they impact upon the identity of the individual. The micro-context interacts with the macro-context and can promote criticism of it or counteract its influence in the life of the individual. For instance, some religious groups try to separate themselves from wider society or change it in some way, in seeking religious goals.

Some theorists of conversion argue that, prior to conversion, the potential convert experiences some acute crisis in their life which opens them to consideration of new ways of organizing themselves and their lives. In this sense conversion has been seen by some as a coping mechanism where existing ones have failed. Crises may occur because of large-scale social change and the erosion of the taken-for-granted ways of living, or because of more micro-level factors such as problems in socialization or in the fulfilment of desires.

The idea of quest is also used in models of conversion by those who conceptualize humans as active creators of meaning in their lives rather than the passive recipients of either fate or social forces. The notion of quest assumes that people are actively involved in a search for meaning and purpose in life, which may become more intense in periods of crisis. In a recent and important study of conversion, Altemeyer and Hunsberger differentiate between 'amazing apostates' and 'amazing believers'. For the former, the quest for truth that leads to apostasy arises out of the converts' rejection not so much of the faith, as of the guardians of it. On the other hand, the latter group may convert for quite different reasons, in which religion provides meaning, solace and salvation in the midst of alienation and apathy.

Another stage of conversion which can be drawn from the literature is that of encounter with the particular religious group. Many factors are analysed surrounding the encounter, such as the setting, demographic characteristics, and congruence between the convert and group, the role and background of the advocate of the religion, and the interaction between them and the potential convert. In the analysis of the encounter, the role of charisma is often important; the way in which the charismatic leader advocates and legitimates the belief system may be considered, along with the relationship between the leader and other members of the group. It has been suggested that charisma can have a large effect on an individual's decision to convert. Groups can be seen to provide solutions to a variety of needs which the individual has, from the need for community in the face of the erosion of the community in wider society, through to religious needs which the individual may experience. Evidence suggests that, in large part, converts may use religious belief systems or ways of life creatively, modifying them to fit their own particular set of needs or aspirations.

Following the initial encounter with the group, continued interaction is important, and is the next stage which can be identified. This allows the potential convert to learn more about the belief systems of the group and its way of life. The length of this period of interaction and its intensity varies between groups. Some advocate a long period of learning and socialization, whilst others may demand a quicker decision from the potential convert and interaction may be more intensive. This is influenced by the degree of contact the group has with the outside world and the views they have of it. Groups in which boundaries with the outside world are flexible may be less controlling of the individual and interaction may be less intense, and the opposite is the case for those groups who separate themselves from the world. A quick decision may be required from a group regarded as deviant by the outside world, for fear that the potential 'convert may be put off by the stigma attached to the group.

During the phase of interaction, personal relationships are particularly important: acceptance and affirmation by those in the group may help to promote conversion and overcome crises. The nature of this interaction and the degree and type of persuasion which operates between groups and converts is a much debated area. Some theorists have cast converts in the role of victims of the irresistible brainwashing techniques of religious groups, asserting that groups pick out vulnerable people and manipulate them by playing on their deepest needs and desires.

The final element of the interaction phase is the need for a public declaration of the decision to convert in many groups. Often anguish and confusion surrounding the adoption of a whole new set of values and ways of living may be alleviated by the public declaration of a decision to convert leading to an experience of divine and group affirmation.

The last stage to be delineated is that of commitment. Religious traditions, through commitment to the new perspective, tend to require a radical rejection of old ways of life and of the world and its 'evil'. Symbols of death and rebirth may be used in the commitment stage, which is characterized by a clear distinction between the 'right' and the 'wrong' way, the inadequacy of past life and the superiority of the religious way of life. Previous life becomes reinterpreted through new frames of reference often assisted by the giving of public testimony. Life experience is gradually rearranged and modified, using the discourse of the group. The giving of testimony has been perceived variously as a precondition for conversion, a result of conversion and a way of adopting the ideology, roles and vocabulary of the group. At the least, testimony is likely to consolidate belief and at the same time it reminds the group of the validity and continued relevance of its world-view.

Many believe that conversion is merely the first step in an ongoing process. Conversion may be moral, intellectual or emotional in the first instance, but it must then come to pervade all aspects of life for the convert to be totally transformed. It is not just a personal change but a reorientation to the world in general. The nature, intensity and duration of conversion affect the consequences in individual cases and it is difficult to make judgements as to the exact degree of change which occurs in each convert.

Conversion may be analysed from a variety of different viewpoints, from a consideration of the religious tradition involved, and the developmental process of the convert within it, to a more social perspective regarding, for example, the extent to which the convert remains within or is alienated from their immediate and wider society. Conversion – as these essays show – is not a unitary phenomenon, but a 'multi-faceted process of change'. Conversion cannot be analysed from any one 'objective' standpoint; it is always to be seen from a particular viewpoint, in which specific ways of theorizing obtain insights, which in turn must be made explicit.

The variety of definitions of conversion extant in both religious and academic writing are an attempt to cover the extensive range of the phenomenon. Within Judaism and Christianity, conversion can signify the rejection of evil and the coming into a relationship with God. This can occur between denominations, converting, for example (in one scenario) from 'Godless and idolatrous' Roman Catholicism to 'true' (Protestant) Christianity. Academic definitions of conversion vary as to the degree of change which takes place in a person, and the amount of time over which it takes place. Some regard it as a sudden change involving radical alterations in belief, behaviour and group membership. Others see it as more gradual and developmental, and not as all-encompassing of a person's life.

Equally, the subject of conversion – as an area for theology and religious studies – has often presupposed that 'conversion' is an individualistic narrative of change. However, it has taken a century or more of missiology to show that conversion is more complex. Vincent Donovan's moving account of the baptism of the Masai explores the more subtle phenomenon of communities in conversion. Donovan, working within an individualistic (and Western?) paradigm of conversion, attempts to baptize only those members of the tribe that have played a full part in his instruction courses. But Ndangoya, a tribal elder, will have none of it:

> 'Padri, why are you trying to break us up and separate us? ... there have been lazy ones in this community. But they have been helped by those with much energy. There are stupid ones in the community, but they have been helped by those who are intelligent. Yes, there are ones with little faith in this village, but they have been helped by those with much faith ... I can declare for them and for all this community, that we have rached the step in our lives where we can say "We believe".' (Donovan 1982, p. 91)

Donovan agrees to baptize the whole tribe: 'conversion' is a communal phenomenon, no longer individuals responding in their 'own' time.

Missiology still has much to render to the study of conversion; increasingly, so does sociology. Grace Davie has recently characterized the story of religious affiliation in post-war Britain as 'believing without belonging' (*Religion in Britain since 1945* (Clarendon Press, 1995)). The thesis itself raises further questions for the study of conversion. How do church members define themselves? What is the difference between being religious and spiritual? If there is an apparent decline in the number of converts – perhaps perceived because there are fewer large-scale Christian rallies (e.g. those of Billy Graham, Luis Palau and others), does that make Britain a less religious place? If millions attend Alpha courses, does that mean there are, in fact, now more converts? The answers are far from clear.

The study of conversion is the study of change. Yet even here, the study takes place in a context ('religious' and 'social') in which change is a constant. The claim to be 'born again' carries a different weight of significance in British evangelical churches now, compared with only twenty years ago. Not so long ago the claim, and its meanings, were largely uncontested within evangelical circles. But successive revolutions – Charismatic Renewal, Post-evangelicalism and neo-Conservative evangelicalism, to name but a few movements – would all now claim to or wish to qualify such a statement. Suffice to say, much of the concern would centre on the significance of religious experience in relation to 'basic' doctrine.

This introduction attempts to show how complex the study of conversion is. No one discipline can comprehensively investigate and interpret the phenomenon. So the future of the study is likely to lie in more inter-disciplinary work, with increasing emphasis given to the rapid developments that are taking place within many religious systems at the turn of the millennium. Part of that work will be giving more space to the emerging narratives of change, as patterns of conversion develop. Readers, authors, scholars and students can be helped by beginning some of their reflection here.

References and Further Reading

Altemeyer, B. and Hunsberger, B. (1997), *Amazing Conversions: Why Some Turn to Faith and Others Abandon Religion*, Amherst, NY: Prometheus Books.

Donovan, V. (1982), *Christianity Rediscovered: An Epistle from the Masai*, London: SCM Press.

Nock, A. D. (1933), *Conversion: The Old and the New in Religion from Alexander the Great to Augustine of Hippo*, Oxford: Clarendon Press.

Rambo, L. (1987), 'Conversion' in Eliade, M. (ed.), *The Encyclopaedia of Religion*, London: Macmillan.

Rambo, L. (1993), *Understanding Religious Conversion*, New Haven, CT: Yale University Press.

Robertson, R. (1978), *Meaning and Change*, Oxford: Clarendon Press.

Thanks also to Louise Goodwin for help in the preparation of this chapter.

Chapter One

A PSYCHOLOGY OF CONVERSION – FROM ALL ANGLES

Sara Savage

The study of conversion is like the proverbial elephant described from various 'blind' perspectives: a perplexing, hodgepodge of a creature. From whatever angle we psychologists view conversion, we 'see' only in part. Still, we have to begin somewhere, and the early psychologists made a credible start. William James was fascinated by the swathe of conversions in the early part of the twentieth century. In 1902, drawing on published spiritual biographies and other personal documents, James described the conversion experience:

> To be converted, to be regenerated, to receive grace, to experience religion, to gain an assurance, (these) are so many phrases which denote the process, gradual or sudden, by which a self hitherto divided, and consciously wrong, inferior and unhappy, becomes unified and consciously right, superior and happy, in consequence of its firmer hold upon religious realities. This at least is what conversion signifies in general terms, whether or not we believe that a direct divine operation is needed to bring such a moral change about. (James 1958, p. 157)

Since James, psychologists have sought to abstract and describe what goes on in conversion. In 1916, Coe described some criteria of conversion that still ring true today. Conversion is understood as:

- the transformation of the self;
- that comes through some definite process, not just personal maturation;
- has radical consequences for how people think, feel and behave;
- is in some 'higher' direction;
- occurs in a social context.

1

This chapter will explore various psychological angles on conversion. But first a health warning. Conversion described by psychologists stands in stark contrast to theologians' or converts' descriptions. It may strike one as odd that the psychology of conversion reveals very little about the workings of God in the human soul. Isn't that what conversion is all about? So what can psychology say that is of any value? Two factors must be borne in mind. First of all, psychology as a.1 empirical science can report only what is observable (either through direct observation or through what people *say* they have experienced). Also, the psychology of conversion is itself part of a larger 'conversation'. It is a response (possibly uninvited) to those who claim conversion is 'nothing but' the action of the divine upon the searching, needy individual. Psychologists (and sociologists) say in return, 'Not so – here is evidence of psychological and social processes that on their own can go a long way to explain what you "insiders" call conversion.' So who is right? I declare my own position by affirming with 'insiders' that yes, conversion is an encounter with the divine. As a psychologist, I am also convinced that powerful psychological and social processes are present. I argue that the social sciences provide a valuable, but incomplete, angle on conversion. In reality, conversion is probably a case of double causality, both social-psychological and divine, a mystery whose disentangling lies beyond the scope of this chapter. For now we will have to settle for what psychologists have *observed* about conversion in nearly one hundred years of research.

One summarizing statement can be made of this vast literature: there is very little agreement on what conversion looks like. Like the 'blind guides' describing the elephant, each study seems to have got hold of a different part of the animal. Rather than attempt a comprehensive review, my method in this chapter is to highlight, with examples, the main tensions that run throughout the range of studies. Many of these tensions were first identified in James's early, insightful study, while others have emerged more recently. These tensions, or points of disagreement about conversion, can be described as:

- sudden conversion vs gradual conversion;
- adolescent conversion vs mid-life conversion;
- conversion preceded by crisis vs no crisis;
- conversion as passive vs conversion as active;
- negative mental health outcomes vs positive mental health outcomes;
- conversion as socially constructed vs spiritually inspired;
- the individual self as goal vs self-in-relationship as goal.

Conversion: Sudden or Gradual?

With St Paul's Damascus road experience serving as a prototype for Christian conversion, early psychologists concentrated on 'sudden' conversions. Richardson (1985, pp. 164–6) describes the 'old Damascus road' paradigm in which conversion:

- occurs suddenly;
- is emotional (more than rational);
- is felt to be due to external forces acting on a passive recipient;
- is followed by dramatic transformation of self;
- shows behaviour change following belief change;
- occurs once and is permanent;
- occurs in adolescence.

In the earlier part of the twentieth century, these conversions were accompanied by an acute sense of sin and guilt. This appears today to be recast as 'need' – as emotional or social need, or as existential need (spiritual hunger, emptiness, purposelessness and the need for identity). Why the concept of sin has become very unpopular is itself interesting. Undoubtedly the interpretive framework that surrounds the idea of sin (an angry God, rigid puritanical standards that evoke feelings of unworthiness) do not 'resonate' with the norms and goals of our consumer culture. And so the 'paradigm' of sudden conversion may be at odds with current social and religious norms. This is important. According to Rambo's study of conversion, 'consonance of core values and symbols [between the cultural context and the new religion] will facilitate conversion' (1993, p. 42). Nevertheless, many researchers have noted the way St Paul's conversion has been, and often continues to be, institutionalized as the preferred way of entering the Christian faith. This is what evangelistic outreach campaigns often try to elicit. 'Before and after' contrasts are expected in testimonies of Christian conversion. Evangelical churches seem to require evidence of a 'born again' experience which can be tied down to a specific point in time.

In contrast, sociological research has shown that many people who respond to evangelistic altar calls are not 'technically' experiencing conversion, but rather an intensification of previously held beliefs. This is a valuable experience in itself, but it is not the 'sudden' conversion that is hoped for. Sudden conversions have been thought to be the precursors of greater religious commitment; hence they are sought for as the mark of being a 'real' Christian. In fact, Liu (1991) found that it is a conscious commitment, not a 'sudden' conversion experience, that promotes religious devotion. Liu compared religious commitment following sudden and gradual

conversions. Commitment was measured in terms of identity commitment and resource commitment (time, activity and money).
His results showed there was no difference in terms of commitment
between sudden or gradual converts. What does make a difference
is making a conscious commitment at some point, whether that
process was sudden or gradual. Christians who had remained
within the faith that they had been raised in without ever making a
conscious decision were apparently less committed to their faith. In
this sense, the traditional 'altar call' as an opportunity to voice commitment can be helpful, providing such events are not overly pre-
scriptive about what conversion should look like.

Even if conversion appears sudden, there are usually precursors.
Allier, in his *Psychologie de la conversion chez les peuples non-civilisés*
(1925) asserts 'the number of conversions provoked by dreams is incalculable' (Allier 1925, pp. 373–4). He provides accounts of, for instance, tribal chieftains who were 'prepared' in advance of hearing
the message of missionaries through dreams or inner intimations.
More recent studies of conversion have shown that most conversions
are in fact gradual. Stark and Bainbridge (1980) place great emphasis on the social networks and relationships that form between a potential convert and a religious group. They claim it is interpersonal
involvement that leads a person gradually to accept the beliefs of
those people he or she has come to trust.

This is true of conversions to any religion, Christian or otherwise.
As sociologists wrestled with why people were joining cults (New
Religious Movements, NRMs), the earlier 'brainwashing' explanation was replaced with a 'social drift' model. Rather than potential
converts being 'forced' through manipulative techniques to
believe, it was found that in reality they gradually 'drifted' into conversion almost imperceptibly, even inadvertently, through the influence of social relationships. Although Christians like to think of
Christian conversion as qualitatively different from conversion to
another religion, contemporary approaches to Christian evangelism place a similar emphasis on friendship networks. This is partly
in recognition that styles of conversion have changed in recent
decades, and that people are in general reluctant to be persuaded
to make an 'instant' decision for Christ. It recognizes that people
need time to explore new beliefs and test their reality in the context
of relationship. The ten-week Alpha course, in which information
about the Christian faith is shared in a friendly environment, has deliberately harnessed this factor in the conversion process. Undoubtedly this explains some of its appeal. As well, the style of Alpha is
more socially acceptable than the classic revivalist meeting.
Rather than potential converts facing an embarrassingly public

and emotional event, Alpha provides a soothingly middle-class dinner-party type of setting for the exploration of the Christian faith. Alpha wisely recognizes (or perhaps has stumbled upon the truism) that conversion is as much a social process as it is an individual decision, whether sudden or gradual.

Conversion: in Adolescence or in Middle Age?

A second tension running through conversion studies regards the age at which conversion is most likely to occur. Over forty years of correlating age with conversion, researchers have found that mid-adolescence is the peak time (Hood *et al.* 1996). Admittedly, researchers expected that to be the case, and the age range of the typical sample was narrow. Nevertheless, it is a consistent finding that the average age of conversion is around 15.2 years of age (Johnson 1959). Why? Many things are happening at once for teenagers. Their intellectual capacity has suddenly mushroomed. There is plenty of evidence to support Piaget's (1962) theory of children's cognitive development that the capacity to think in terms of abstract logic (called formal operations) does not occur until around the age of 12. With the advent of abstract thought, the great existential questions of life can begin knocking on the door: Who am I? Why am I here? How should I relate to others? What happens when I die? Adolescents begin to enjoy, or fight for, emancipation from parental control: they face the prospect of carving out their own identities, careers and purpose in life. Teenagers have less to lose, and more to gain, by opening themselves to new experiences. As hormones are racing, so moral issues about sex, relationships and responsibility hover in the background. Religious faith as a way of addressing the existential questions of life can become attractive, even in the face of anti-religious peer pressure. As well, the struggle for personal formation can also lead youngsters to de-convert from the faith they were raised in: adolescence is also a peak time for church-leaving. The teenage years are not surprisingly a time of great change. Now in the UK, the average age has risen to 18.11 (Brierley and Wraight 1997). This does not necessarily suggest that the picture is much different – 70 per cent of converts are under the age of 20. The rise in average age may result from the increased number of adult converts who are newcomers to the charismatic house-churches (harvested, quite frequently, from existing mainline churches). As the churches lose more members among the late teens and early twenties group than any other, Brierley suggests that churches would do well to invest in this volatile age group.

The conversion statistics contrast sharply with Jung's theory (based on extensive clinical experience) that religious development is the task and prerogative of middle age. The first half of life, according to Jung, is taken up with the challenge of developing one's ego-identity, and coming to grips with the demands of the real world (Ulanov in Young-Eisendrath and Dawson 1997). It is about skill learning, relationship forming, earning one's bread and butter. In the first half of life it is easy to live largely in terms of the 'persona', the image or mask we present to the world, the self that has been socialized to be acceptable. Jung observed that his clients, especially in mid life, often experienced something akin to a call. This call could be totally disruptive, occurring through emotional and mental upheaval. It was a call to become more than just the socially acceptable mask, to become more authentic, to grow beyond ego-consciousness and to become connected to the transcendent realm. The purpose of life, Jung declared, is essentially religious, yet most of us only have the time and maturity to respond to that call in mature adulthood.

The neo-Freudian psychologist Erickson also found later adult life as a time of reckoning. Erickson's (1982) eighth and final stage of development presents adults with a crisis of integrity (wholeness, synthesis, spiritual values) versus a crisis of despair (in the face of the finitude of life). Erickson believed that as in the physical development of embryos, humans have a psychological drive to develop fully over the entire life span. His theory of psycho-social development states that when the bulk of life's activity is past, the main task of later adulthood is to integrate and make sense of one's life, to resolve life's unfinished business. Like Jung, Erickson developed his theories through clinical practice. These theories, along with many spiritual biographies, indicate that the religious quest is not confined to adolescence, but can come at any point in life. Adolescence and mid-to-later adult life seem to be 'natural' points of existential questioning, although this questioning probably takes a different form in later life. Later religious awakening is not as often experienced as a 'radical conversion', but rather comprises an intensification of nominally held beliefs. But the effects of such an intensification may be even more profound and long-lasting than sudden adolescent conversions, some of which are noticeably temporary. Conn's (1986) lifelong developmental approach to conversion is particularly useful as a research paradigm here. However, the adolescent peak is probably more easily *observed*, not least because of the spiky contours of adolescent convictions.

Conversion: Preceded by Crisis or No Crisis?

The 'old' paradigm of conversion in psychological research expected to see a crisis, or some kind of extreme psychological distress, prior to the conversion. Indeed there was much evidence for this in the early research of Starbuck, James and others. More recently, Ullman (1982) studied the conversion process among converts to Bahai, Judaism, Buddhism and Roman Catholicism. The converts, in contrast to those who were lifelong members of a faith community, all had experienced emotionally difficult relationships in childhood, adolescence, and just prior to their own conversion. At a statistically significant level, Ullman found that the converts had weak, absent or cruel fathers, and that forming a strong emotional tie to the guru, priest or rabbi was a crucial part of the conversion process. One reading of this data may suggest that the conversion was motivated out of emotional need, and the fulfilling of this need occurred within a social relationship.

The view that a crisis precedes conversion can seem to fall into the lap of Freudian attitudes towards religion. Freud saw religious belief as an infantile compensation for the harshness of life, an illusory way of protecting oneself against one's own helplessness. Therefore, in the eyes of some researchers, conversion can be a symptom of psychological weakness, evident in the pre-conversion crisis. Kirkpatrick and Shaver (1990) report that people who had a weak or distant bond with their own mothers are more likely to have a sudden conversion and then develop a close, intense relationship with God (cited in Loewenthal 1995). Are such conversions a pathological compensation for emotional deprivation? Another way of interpreting this data is to see conversion as an overcoming of previous failed attachment, rather than as a compensation. In pastoral practice, Fraser Watts[1] has observed that people's image of God and style of religion more often *reflects* their basic outlook on life rather than compensating for it. For example, it is more natural for a person who experienced a punitive, rejecting father to see God in similar tones, rather than as a compensatory warm, forgiving and all-loving God.

Rambo (1993) attempts to be true to the experiences of converts. He presents a seven-stage sequential model that involves crisis in the early stages.[2] Rambo argues that although some sort of crisis does precede conversion, it can be a slow, cumulative process where 'a final straw breaks the camel's back'. To outsiders, the 'straw' may indeed appear trivial. Diluting the argument even further, Heinrich (1977) compared Roman Catholic charismatics with a control group of non-charismatic Roman Catholics and found that *both* groups reported stress. Heinrich concludes that stress or crisis alone is insufficient to predict conversion: stress is just too common an experience. If stress were sufficient to foment conversion, all would be converted!

How one speaks about one's level of stress or lack of it prior to conversion is undoubtedly shaped by the expectations of one's social milieu. Many conversion testimonies suggest this. In more conservative circles, the awfulness of the pre-conversion state is contrasted with the bliss of the post-conversion state. Even a sheltered adolescent raised in a strict evangelical church and family may feel a need to blacken her relatively protected but pre-conversion past. Researchers interested in the way our use of language can shape what we experience have rightly pointed out that there is a degree of 'construction' in such testimonies. It is possible that the case for a crisis before conversion is overstated. On the other hand, a theological perspective would argue that all human beings, whatever the vagaries of their socio-economic background, have existential needs (for forgiveness, for eternal life, for relationship with God and others) and that this inescapable need is a fundamental ingredient of the conversion process. Conn argues that conversion is not pathologically need-driven, it is not an 'aberrant process but ... one integrated into healthy human growth and quest' (Rambo 1993, p. 64).

The argument over whether a crisis precedes conversion in my opinion has to do with felt need, and expressed need. Felt need is not so much deprivation in comparison with those around, as deprivation relative to one's own expectations of life, and what one is prepared to admit to, first to oneself, and then to others. With these variables, there is much room for manoeuvre. What does seem to be certain is that people are more likely to admit to their (prior) existential needs after conversion. At the very least, conversion, and the new religious community, gives one tacit permission (and perhaps encouragement) to do so.

Conversion: Is the Convert Passive or Active?

Early studies of conversion which focused on the mystical Damascus road conversion experience speak of a passive submission to an ineffable sense of 'presence':

> ... a sense of sudden understanding accompanied by a feeling of elation and by an auditory and sometimes visual hallucination ... There is a feeling of change within the self ... associated with a sense of presence. (Christensen 1963, p. 214)

Although with a strictly 'mystical' type of conversion there is no social pressure, the conversion is experienced as something that happens to the passive person.

Lofland and Skonovd (1981) have organized a variety of conversion experiences in terms of six different conversion motifs (see Table 1). These motifs can each be located on the passive–active spectrum. At least two types of conversion show high levels of social pressure: revivalist and coercive.

> The 'social pressure' and 'contagion' (of revivalist campaigns) – albeit brief – can produce fear, guilt, and joy of such intensity that individuals may obediently go through the outward and inward methodology of a fundamentalist or evangelical conversion. (Lofland in press, quoted in Lofland and Skonovd 1981, p. 381)

These sorts of revivalist campaigns have lost credibility to some extent, partly because of social change. As well, some research into the effectiveness of evangelism has shown that rather than achieving lasting conversion, many who go forward for an altar call are either intensifying nominally held beliefs, or may be trying to recapture and relive a previous conversion experience.

Overtly coercive conversion is extremely rare in Christianity, although the possibility of social psychological coercion over time is real. What is ironic is that the conversion itself may have occurred in a relatively unpressured manner, but with some religious groups, the intense commitment required after conversion may so constrain a person's social world and the cognitive tools needed to interpret

| | Conversion motifs | | | | | |
	intellectual	mystical	experimental	affectional	revivalist	coercive
degree of social pressure	low or none	little or none	low	medium	high	high
temporal duration of conversion experience	medium	short	long	long	short	long
level of affective arousal	medium	high	low	medium	high	high
affective content	illumination	awe, love, fear	curiosity	affection	love and (fear)	fear and (love)
belief-participation sequence	belief-participation	belief-participation	participation-belief	participation-belief	participation-belief	participation-belief

Table 1   (From Lofland and Skonovd).

that world, that post-conversion reality is in practice defined by the group.

With the affectional type of conversion, there is a medium amount of social pressure. Affectional conversion relies on the importance of relationships formed with the new religious community: 'interpersonal bonds are the fundamental support for recruitment' (Stark and Bainbridge 1980, p. 389). Personal affect (emotion), trust, and respect for the practising believers are vital for the conversion process. There is a large body of research that indicates the prevalence of this type of conversion.

In contrast to the view that the convert is a passive recipient of either divine or social pressure, a number of researchers give an 'activist' model of conversion (Lofland 1977, Lofland and Skonovd 1981, Strauss 1976, Richardson 1979). Richardson (1985) sees the potential convert as an active meaning-seeker. In Lofland and Skonovd's (1981) model, two types of conversion motifs can be considered to be free of social influence: the intellectual and the experimental. The intellectual type serves as a pure 'activist' form of conversion. 'Intellectual' conversion may be arrived at through reading, television, lectures and other non-interactive methods of enquiring about a faith. With intellectual conversion there is little or no social pressure, the searching and eventual conversion may happen over a medium length of time, emotional arousal is tame, and belief precedes participation. The individuals, as it were, 'convert' themselves. With the increasingly privatized nature of religion and of contemporary life in general, Lofland and Skonovd feel this relatively rare type of conversion may be on the increase.

The experimental type of conversion is motivated largely by curiosity. Lofland and Skonovd suggest that this happens to a surprising degree. People begin with a pragmatic 'show me' attitude, and try on the new religion like a pair of shoes. After trying it out, a decision may be gradually made. Social pressure is not directly involved, but certainly there would be a shaping of social reality by the new religious community.

Although Kilbourne and Richardson (1989) point out that the different types of conversion motifs, rather than representing historically shifting forms of conversion, may actually result more from the differing emphases of researchers (who select different aspects of the conversion experience), it is hard to disentangle such an argument because all research proceeds from an a priori theory which highlights some features more than others. However, one could also question why certain aspects of conversion were salient to researchers at a specific time and not others. Might this not also be an indication of 'the spirit of the times'? In brief, there appears currently to be more than one route to conversion, with revivalist and coercive forms as fairly unpopular choices, while affectional, intellectual and experimental forms seem to be on the increase. These latter three have in common a more active role (medium to high) for the potential convert over a period of seeking (medium to long). At the very least such routes to conversion show greater consonance with the values of our consumer society.

Conversion: Negative Mental Health Outcomes or Positive Mental Health Outcomes?

From the way conversion testimonies are structured, one would expect that individuals' pre-conversion mental states would show more depression, anxiety and stress. Unfortunately this is very hard to demonstrate. First, the rarity of studies that assess the pre-conversion state means there is little if any hard evidence of significant mental disturbance for individuals before conversion relative to the general population (see Loewenthal 1995). Certainly converts report more unhappiness prior to their conversions compared with their post-conversion state, as suggested earlier. Converts' retrospective accounts may somewhat conform to their expectations of what their experience ought to be; they are now 'ready' to see the unhappiness of their former lives. In fact this may be part of the conversion process itself: people come to see themselves in terms of a new and better identity compared to the former self which in James's (1902) words was 'wrong, inferior and unhappy'.

It is, therefore, difficult to establish an objective 'baseline' of typical mental health prior to conversion. There are, however, many studies that measure mental health after conversion. Loewenthal suggests the following sequence is often experienced:

> Converts start off in a sad way (or so they say), get helped by their conversion, but possibly may relapse under the pressures of assimilating to the new social world and new beliefs, and working out a viable lifestyle. (1995, p. 72)

It is possible that this sequence makes sense of some contradictory findings about mental health after conversion. For instance, Stanley (1964) found that the sudden conversion of some theology students resulted in lower neuroticism scores (i.e. the sudden converts had better mental health in terms of neuroticism), while Allison (1967) found that sudden converts were higher on anxiety than gradual converts. As anxiety and neuroticism are usually related, these findings seem contradictory. It may be that the young theology student sudden converts were still in the flush of their post-conversion 'honeymoon', while the other study tapped into a later post-conversion stage.

More generally, there is a huge volume of studies that seek to measure the mental health outcomes of religious faith. Although these are not strictly conversion studies, they have some bearing on our present topic. Batson and Ventis (1982) reviewed 57 such studies and found that, on the whole, having a religious faith is good for your mental health. However, different ways of being religious showed different mental health outcomes. Batson and Ventis distinguished between three styles of being religious: extrinsic religiosity, intrinsic religiosity and 'Quest'. Allport and Ross (1967) defined the extrinsic individual as the person who *uses* their religion for their own self-serving ends, such as security, solace, status, sociability. The intrinsic individual embraces a creed, internalizes it, and attempts to follow it fully. 'It is in this sense that he *lives* his religion' (Allport and Ross 1967, p. 434). The general findings suggest that extrinsic and intrinsic religiousness represent different motives for religious belief which are largely independent of each other. Quest, the third religious style, is defined by Batson, Schoenrade and Ventis (1993) as readiness to face existential questions without reducing their complexity, self-criticism, perception of religious doubt as positive, and openness to change. In their analysis of the 57 mental health studies, Batson and Ventis (1982) found that the much vaunted claim that religion is a mark of an immature and weak personality was found to be true only with extrinsic religiosity. Extrinsic religion, as described by Allport, does not

> entail self-objectification, but remains unreflective, failing to provide a context of meaning in which the individual can locate himself. Finally, the immature sentiment is not unifying in its effect on the personality ... Even when fanatic in intensity, it is but partially integrative. (Allport 1950, p. 54)

In contrast, Allport was convinced that intrinsic religiosity was all that was good in religion and would be a powerful contributor to positive mental health. Batson and Ventis found that both Questers and Intrinsics showed positive mental health outcomes, but in different ways. Intrinsic believers, who are firmly committed to their religion, showed freedom from guilt, freedom from existential anxieties and freedom from the fear of death. Persons high on Quest showed a greater sense of self-acceptance and self-actualization, and more self-reliance in comparison with Intrinsics who showed higher reliance on God. It is hard to say which orientation, that of Questers or that of Intrinsics, had the 'healthier' outcome; it depends upon

one's prior definition of mental health. Questers may suffer more existential anxiety than Intrinsics. On the other hand, argue Batson
and Ventis, it is possible that the freedom from guilt and worry
gained by Intrinsics is won at the price of 'bondage to belief', commitment to a rigid belief system which cannot be questioned.

Whether conversion results in good mental health or not is really
too complex a question to be answered with a simple yes or no.
Batson and Ventis (1982) liken religious experience (such as conversion, but other religious experience could also qualify) to the process
of creativity. Creativity, they argue, involves an improvement in
one's cognitive organization. A creative change involves a shift to a
more complex, differentiated and integrated view of reality. Piaget's idea of disequilibrium is that creative, cognitive shifts occur
when one's current reality ceases to function effectively, and one is
'forced' to a new vision of reality. Moving from an outmoded, ineffective view of reality to a more creative, integrated one seems to
involve stages which appear to be similar to some of the stages identified in the conversion process: preparation (involving existential
dissatisfaction), incubation (a period where nothing seems to be
happening consciously, although there are indications that there
may be much subconscious mental activity), illumination (aha!)
and verification (trying out the new world-view, participating in
the new community). Conversion may involve a restructuring of
vision in order to deal with the existential questions of life, and as
such it is considered a healthy cognitive advance.

Alternatively, it is possible to get stuck: conversion experiences
which seem to halt the convert in this new vision, forever attempting
to relive that original illumination, may ultimately result in
'bondage to belief'. This accords with Loewenthal (1995) who
argues that it is not so much the conversion experience itself that is
important for mental health, but rather it is the ongoing processes of
personal and religious development that determine the long-term
mental health outcome. Conversion is just a first step along the road.

Socially Constructed – Spiritually Inspired

With this tension we see the greatest degree of conflict between the
religious understandings of conversion in contrast with the empirical approach of the human sciences. Theology makes radical, *pre-
scriptive* claims about conversion: 'for in Christ Jesus you are all
children of God through faith' (Galatians 3.26 NRSV). These
claims concern spiritual, eternal realities, and as such are largely
untestable. Such claims are perhaps only understood within the
faith community. *Descriptions* of conversion from subjective experi-

ence, found in testimonies or spiritual biographies, borrow from theological language. Depending on the social and denominational milieu, they emphasize different aspects of theology to make sense of personal religious experience. These may be prone to exaggeration and selective perception, but many of them resonate with a personal reality that merits respect. In contrast, empirical approaches study only what can be observed: the person in interaction with others. What is experienced as intensely spiritual to those who have undergone conversion appears to sociologists and psychologists the result of social-psychological influences.

Statistical research clearly shows that the religion you are most likely to convert to is the religion which is dominant in your own background and culture (Batson, Ventis and Schoenrade 1983). Is it therefore all down to 'social pressure' or 'social influence'? Conversion appears to happen at fairly predictable life-stages, yet in a variety of ways. It seems that without a social context full conversion would not happen at all (Rambo 1993).

So what is conversion then? Is it simply a change in attitude and beliefs? Some psychologists are focusing on attribution – how people explain the causes of events. For instance, rather than seeing conversion as a radical 'transformation of self', Snow and Malachek (1984) view conversion as a change in discourse, the way we speak about the world. A change in discourse will be accompanied by a shift in consciousness, the way we perceive reality. Prior to conversion, most people have 'secular' explanations for what happens in life. They failed an exam because they did not study. The natural world evolved from single-celled animals. After conversion, attributions change, and God is perceived at the helm of events. Converts develop a 'master' religious attribution, learned from the chosen faith community.

There is no doubt that conversion takes place in a social-historical context and that interpersonal relationships are an intrinsic part of it. Full conversion is unlikely to happen outside of the shaping influence of relationships with fellow believers and participation in their practices and beliefs. We are left with the tension that conversion is socially constructed, and yet 'insiders' believe it is so much more. Unresolvable tensions remain in the wake of conversion studies. I doubt if one can improve upon Rambo's summarizing statement of the tensions covered so far:

> Conversion is paradoxical. It is elusive. It is inconclusive. It destroys and it saves. Conversion is sudden and it is gradual. It is created totally by the action of God, and it is created totally by the action of humans. Conversion is both personal and

communal, private and public. It is both passive and active. It is a retreat from the world. It is a resolution of conflict and an empowerment to go into the world and to confront, if not to create, conflict. Conversion is an event and a process. It is an ending and a beginning. It is final and open-ended. Conversion leaves us devastated – and transformed. (Rambo 1993, p. 76)

Conversion: Is the Individual the Goal or is Relationship the Goal?

I would like to add one final tension to our list. Psychologists and sociologists have sought to understand conversion by abstracting elements that are in common with conversions across religions (including cults). This been done (heretical as it may seem to Christians) in order to avoid the problem of circularity: 'conversion is whatever the faith community says it is'. As fruitful as this abstracting process has been, it has inevitably meant that aspects which are unique to Christianity are overlooked. Along with Rambo (1989), I suggest there needs to be more emphasis on the theological content of conversion in order to make sense of it. The content of beliefs *will* shape what people experience.

One feature of Christian conversion and teaching which is not picked up by the psychological research is the emergence of the self-in-relationship, a participation in the relationship which Jesus enjoys with his Father: 'May they be in us, just as you are in me and I am in you' (John 17.21a GNB). The psychological approach to conversion appears to me to be profoundly individualistic, despite the emphasis on the convert's relationship to the new religious community. The self is still considered a self-contained entity, albeit, after conversion, an improved, gleaming, transformed self. The individual self is the goal of conversion.

Possibly the old model of conversion as something that happens 'to' the passive individual has structured the way psychologists have continued to view it. Even the model of the self as active meaning-seeker has not done much to break the individualistic mould – here the self converts itself. This individualistic model of self in conversion studies lags behind the more social and relational view of self-identity in recent psychology: the self as dyad (a self formed in relationship to another). Object relations theorists, the work of the developmental psychologist Vygotsky (1962), and research in social psychology are presenting us with a dynamic view of the self created and sustained in 'conversation' with another. The foundational ability to grasp that we are a self (an entity differentiated from the rest of the universe), our ability to use language, our ability to think logically, develops through interaction with another person.

A relational understanding of the self seems particularly relevant to Christian conversion. Christian conversion is often today described in terms of being loved, accepted, embraced, forgiven by another Person. This of course reflects our contemporary concern and hunger for intimacy (Storkey 1995) and the existential need for bonds of trust that our global, rationalized, impersonal society fails to fulfil (Giddens 1991). Kathryn Curran[3] (who is currently researching prisoners' experience of conversion in UK prisons) listens to new converts' stories. She reports that the energy and dynamism for personal change come from inmates' newly experienced *relationship* with God. New converts describe a sense of being loved, and of being 'in love', that gives them the energy to make radical and sweeping personal changes in the face of a hostile, demeaning prison culture. As this prisoner has put it:

> God is everything I have ever wanted in my life. I have always wanted love, he has been there, he loves me. I have always wanted a friend, and he has been there, every time I talk with him I get a warm feeling inside me. If I start feeling lonely, he will put an arm around me and he will say 'don't worry – we are in this together'. I know he is so real.

Focusing on relationship provides yet another angle on conversion. At the very least, what converts are focusing on and what is being talked about has changed. This has consequences for the convert's new identity as a self-in-relationship. What follows from that can be a sense of belonging to, and responsibility for, others. Conversion may now be experienced, not so much in terms of a transformed, improved self, but as a self – for perhaps the first time – in relationship with Another.

Notes

1 Taken from a seminar given by Rev. Dr Fraser Watts in March 1998, Psychology and Christian Ministry Seminars.
2 Rambo's (1993) seven stages are: context, crisis, quest, encounter, interaction, commitment and consequences.
3 Kathryn Curran is a doctoral researcher at the Institute of Criminology, University of Cambridge, 7 West Road, Cambridge CB3 9DT.

References and Further Reading

Allier, R. (1925), *La Psychologie de la conversion chez les peuples non-civilisés*, cited in Yates, T. (1998), 'Christian conversion 1902–1993: James to Lewis Rambo', *ANVIL*, Vol. 15 (2), pp. 99–109.

Allison, J. (1967), Adaptive Regression and Intense Religious Experiences', *Journal of Mental and Nervous Disease*, Vol. 145, pp. 452–63.

Allport, G. and Ross, J. (1967), 'Personal Religious Orientation and Prejudice', *Journal of Social Psychology*, Vol. 5, pp. 432–43.

Allport, R. (1950), *The Individual and His Religion, a Psychological Interpretation*, New York: Macmillan.

Batson, C., Schoenrade, P. and Ventis, W. (1993), *Religion and the Individual: A Social-Psychological Perspective*, New York: Oxford University Press.

Batson, C. D. and Ventis, W. L. (1982), *The Religious Experience*, Oxford: Oxford University Press.

Brierley, P. and Wraight, H. (1997), *UK Christian Handbook*, London: Christian Research.

Christensen, C. (1963), 'Religious Conversion', *Archives of General Psychiatry*, Vol. 9, pp. 207–16.

Coe, G. (1916), *The Psychology of Religion*, Chicago: University of Chicago Press.

Conn, W. (1986), *Christian Conversion: A Developmental Interpretation of Autonomy and Surrender*, Mahwah, NJ: Paulist Press.

Erickson, E. (1982), *The Life Cycle Completed: A Review*, New York: W. W. Norton.

Giddens, A. (1991), *Modernity and Self Identity: Self and Society in the Late Modern Age*, Cambridge: Polity Press.

Heinrich, M. (1977), 'Change of Heart: A Test of some Widely Held Theories of Religious Conversion', *American Sociological Review*, Vol. 83, pp. 653–80.

Hood, R. W. Jr, Spilka, B., Hunsberger, B. and Gorsuch, R. (1996), *The Psychology of Religion*, London: The Guilford Press.

James, W. ([1902] 1985), *The Varieties of Religious Experience*, Cambridge, MA: Harvard University Press.

Johnson, P. (1959), *Psychology of Religion* (rev. edn), New York: Abingdon Press.

Kilbourne, B. and Richardson, J. (1989), 'Paradigm Conflict, Types of Conversion, and Conversion Theories', *Sociological Analysis*, 50, pp. 1–21.

Kirkpatrick, L. and Shaver, P. (1990), 'Attachment Theory and Religion: Childhood Attachments, Religious Beliefs and Conversion', *Journal for the Scientific Study of Religion*, Vol. 29, pp. 315–34.

Liu, C. (1991), 'Becoming a Christian Consciously vs. Non-Consciously', *Journal of Psychology and Theology*, Vol. 19 (4), pp. 364–75.

Loewenthal, K. (1995), *Mental Health and Religion*, London: Chapman and Hall.

Lofland, J. (1977), 'Becoming a World-Saver Revisited', *American Sociological Review*, Vol. 30, pp. 862–74.

Lofland, J. and Skonovd, N. (1981), 'Conversion Motifs', *Journal for the Scientific Study of Religion*, Vol. 20 (4), pp. 373–85.

Piaget, J. (1962), 'The Stages of Intellectual Development of the Child', *Bulletin of the Menninger Clinic*, Vol. 26, pp. 120–8. Also reproduced in Munsinger, H. (ed.) (1975), *Readings in Child Development* (2nd edn), New York: Holt, Reinhart and Winston, pp. 124–30.

Rambo, L. (1989), 'Conversion: Towards a Holistic Model of Religious Change', *Pastoral Psychology*, Vol. 38, pp. 47–63.

Rambo, L. (1993), *Understanding Religious Conversion*, New Haven, CT: Yale University Press.

Richardson, J. (1979), 'A New Paradigm for Conversion Research'. Paper presented at the Annual Meeting of the International Society for Political Psychology.

Richardson, J. (1985), 'The Active vs. Passive Convert: Paradigm Conflict in Conversion/Recruitment Research', *Journal for the Scientific Study of Religion*, Vol. 24, pp. 163–79.

Snow, D. and Malachek, R. (1984), 'The Sociology of Conversion', *Annual Review of Sociology*, Vol. 10, pp. 167–90.

Stanley, G. (1964), 'Personality and Attitude Correlates of Religious Conversion', *Journal for the Scientific Study of Religion*, Vol. 4, pp. 60–63.

Stark, R. and Bainbridge, W. (1980), 'Networks of Faith: Interpersonal Bonds and Recruitment to Cults and Sects', *American Journal of Sociology*, Vol. 85, pp. 1376–1395.

Storkey, E. (1995), *The Search for Intimacy*, London: Hodder and Stoughton.

Strauss, R. (1976), 'Changing Oneself: Seekers and the Creative Transformation of Experience' in Lofland, J., *Doing Social Life*, New York: Wiley, pp. 252–72.

Ulanov, A. (1997), 'Jung and Religion: The Opposing Self' in Young-Eisendrath, P. and Dawson, T. (eds) (1997), *The Cambridge Companion to Jung*, Cambridge: Cambridge University Press, pp. 296–314.

Ullman, C. (1982), 'Cognitive and Emotional Antecedents of Religious Conversion', *Journal of Personality and Social Psychology*, Vol. 43, pp. 183–92.

Vygotsky, L. ([1934] 1962), *Thought and Language* (2nd edn), Cambridge, MA: MIT Press.

Young-Eisendrath, P. and Dawson, T. (eds) (1997), *The Cambridge Companion to Jung*, Cambridge: Cambridge University Press.

Chapter Two

FROM FAITH TO FAITH

Hugh Montefiore

I became a Christian at the age of 16 while I was at a residential school, and only at home for the holidays. Then after a year away at the university, the war broke out, and so I was again away from home; and as soon as I was demobilized I got married. So in these circumstances I was somewhat shielded from the cultural trauma which many can suffer in changing from one faith to another. Further, I don't even think of myself as *changing* my faith so much as *adding* my Christian faith to my Jewish inheritance. In fact I am glad to think of myself as a Jewish Christian. While there are some important differences between Judaism and Christianity, the similarities are even more important. Then, even more importantly, I did not decide to convert: it was decided for me. To put it simply, when sitting alone in my study at school I had a vision of a figure in white accompanied by the words 'Follow me', and I instinctively knew it was Jesus – don't ask me how, as I had never read the New Testament or been involved in any Christian worship or even discussed Christianity with anyone. The event was self-authenticating, and took over my life. It seemed to me that the only way I could obey such a call was to join with other followers of Jesus; and that meant being a member of the Christian Church. That was it. It was as clear cut as that.

Consider the various ways in which Judaism could be related to Christianity. We might hold that all religions are equal, all equally valid ways of approaching God. But that would not account for their differences. Of course, if we thought that there is no God, all religions would be equally false; but we are not atheists. It is sometimes said that Christianity is for Gentiles, while Judaism is for Jews. (Jews do not think that the Jewish laws need to be imposed on Gentiles.) That will not do. How about myself? Had I no right, as a Jew, to become a Christian? Jesus was Jewish: all his disciples were Jews, Christianity started out as a Jewish sect. How could

Jesus have spent his ministry preaching exclusively to Jews if his gospel is intended for Gentiles?

The common view among Christians until quite recently is that Judaism is a dead end, and has been superseded by Christianity. This was the view of the early Church, pointing as proof to the capture of the Jewish temple in Jerusalem by the Romans in AD 70. The Jews, they said, were deicides, that is, killers of God, for they put to death the Son of God. The Jews were cursed by God. But the Jews did not put Jesus to death: he was killed by the Romans at the instigation of the High Priest who himself was appointed by the Romans. There were a few Jews who were culpable; but in no sense could the whole race of the Jews be blamed, let alone those who came after. Anyone who knows anything about Jewish spirituality knows that Jews are not cursed by God: Judaism is a live and vital religion, and many Jews are devoted to God, and show more love and charity than many so-called Christians, as I have learnt from experience.

Nonetheless there are still Christians who believe that Judaism is a dead end. They hold a view called 'supersessionalism', according to which the new covenant ratified in the sacrifice of Jesus superseded the old covenant which God made with Abraham. There were certainly two covenants, but Jesus himself never implied that he had done away with the convenant with Abraham; nor is this stated in the Epistles of St Paul or in the Epistle to the Hebrews. Are then the Jews still the chosen people of God? *Of course they are.* God chose them, and as St Paul wrote, 'the gifts and the calling of God are irrevocable' (Romans 11.29 NRSV). They still have a part to play in the providence of God. As St Paul wrote, if they had not rejected Jesus as Messiah, the gospel would not have spread to the pagan world: it would have remained a sect of Judaism. So then there is a sense in which the Jews' rejection of Christ has been turned into a blessing for the rest of the world. Where does this leave the Church of God? Of course the Church is also part of God's providence, and Christians too are the children of God. We have to say that Jews and Christians are together the elect people of God. Judaism is a religion in its own right; but it is fulfilled by the Christian gospel. What was promised under the old covenant has been fulfilled under the new covenant. I am not alone in saying this. Let me quote the words of the World Council of Churches:

> We believe that in Jesus Christ God's revelation in the Old Testament finds its fulfilment. Through him we see into the very heart of God: we see what it really means to say that God is the God of the covenant and loves man to the very end. As he became the

man who was the perfect instrument of God's purpose, he took upon himself the vocation of his people. As its representative he fulfils Israel's task of obedience. In his resurrection it has become manifest that God's love is stronger than human sin. In him God has forgiven and wiped out sin and in him created his true covenant partner.

I hope, therefore, that you will understand what I mean when I say that I am both Jewish and Christian. This means that it was not all that difficult to go from the one faith to the other. If the two faiths are Judaism and Christianity, and if a person holds the sort of views that I do, the main problem is social and cultural, as I shall explain.

I realize that it will seem to some that I am only playing with words when I say that I am still a Jew. To Jews I am *meshummad*, a traitor, because I have been baptized and become a Christian. To most Christians I will be perceived as having moved from one faith to the other. I certainly do not class myself as a Messianic Jew, that is to say, with those who consider themselves as primarily Jews but who believe not that the Messiah is still to come but that he has already come. I do not join myself with them for two reasons. Most of them are fundamentalists, and, while I have no objection whatsoever to joining in worship with fundamentalists, I cannot belong to a congregation that is fundamentalist *in principle*. Second, I believe that Jesus Christ has 'broken down the middle wall of partition' between Jews and Gentiles, and therefore I need to worship both with Jewish Christians and with Gentile Christians, and not in a purely Jewish Christian milieu as Messianic Jews do. They are rapidly growing in numbers in the USA, and have congregations here in Britain, and in Israel. There have been some attempts earlier to form Jewish Christian churches, in this country by Paul Levertoff, a learned rabbi who became a priest of the Church of England, and Vicar of Holy Trinity, Shoreditch, at a time when most of the parish were Jewish immigrants. These Jewish Christian churches have all failed, partly because they have depended on the dynamic leadership of one man, and partly because they had no real connection with the ongoing holy catholic Church. They may appeal to the individual, but we have to face the fact that, although Christian missions to Jews in the last century were more successful than to any other ethnic group, Jews as a whole have overwhelmingly rejected Christianity – with good reason.

I was fortunate to be born into a loving and religious family. My parents did not disown me when I became a Christian, and I look back on Judaism with great affection. Although in this lecture I shall concentrate on differences between Judaism and Christianity, I must emphasize that the two religions have far more in common than in what they disagree. We have a common commitment to the living God who is the creator of the universe and our redeemer and sanctifier. We have a common conviction that men and women are made in the image of God and therefore always to be respected and honoured. We have a common belief that God created the world and that we human beings have a duty to care for it and not to wreck it. There is a common conviction that the Holy Spirit of God guides humankind. There is a common belief that life will finally be transformed. In all these matters Judaism and Christianity can and should go hand in hand, living as we do today in a near-secular society. Let us not forget that what we call the Old Testament is really the Jewish Bible. The Church has been tempted from its earliest days to reject it, notably by Marcion; but the temptation has always been resisted because it forms a vital part of the Bible, although, alas, it seems seldom to be read aloud in the Church of England today, even though provision is made for it in the Eucharist.

It is from the Jewish Bible that Jesus took what he called the two 'great commandments', and he said that on these hang all the law and the prophets – in other words, they form the foundation of ethical behaviour. We have taken over the Jewish hymn-book, and we use it as our psalms, even if some of them are wildly unsuitable. In matters of faith, ethics and worship there is a close convergence between Judaism and Christianity. But when we look back over past history we find that this convergence has been the cause not of mutual understanding, but of persecution and even of hatred; first on the part of the Jews in the first century when they were dominant, and then for century after century by the Christian Church when it had the power. The two faiths were rivals, and so it was thought necessary to blacken the one in order to benefit the other. I am sorry to have to say this, but it needs to be said.

This terrible record of the treatment of Jews at the hands of Christians when they had the power is the reason why for Jews the name of Jesus Christ is not good news, but bad news. Still in the folk memory are centuries of discrimination, all kinds of indignities: apartheid, oppression, violence, removal of elementary human rights, even burning and death.[1] I am not now referring to the horrors of the Holocaust at the hands of the Nazis. That was secular persecution, although racial anti-Semitism could never have taken hold without the Church's religious anti-Judaism. The biggest hurdle which a Jew has to face when he moves from the one faith to the other is this terrible past history, and it is far more terrible than most Christians realize. That is why Jews found so inadequate the recent statement from the Vatican about the past attitude of the Roman Catholic Church towards the Jews. They felt rather the same as former British prisoners of war in Burma felt when the Emperor of Japan said recently that he felt sadness at the scars of war. The expressions of regret were rather similar in both cases.

In the light of this, it is hardly surprising that when a person changes from Judaism to Christianity, in the eyes of Jews he has gone over to the enemy. Baptism is the key point for Jews. It does not matter so much what a person believes in his heart – how does anyone really know that? – but baptism is a public act, it is an outward profession of faith, something in their eyes akin to circumcision, an unrepeatable act. It also may call to mind in the Jewish folk memory how in the nineteenth century in Germany a Jew could not accept a university chair or an army commission unless he was baptized, and this leads people to the suspicion that people may be baptized for their personal advancement. Or there may be folk memories of forcible baptisms, which have happened at times, or of the requirement of Ferdinand and Isabella at the time of the Inquisition that Jews must either be baptized or leave Spain, an early attempt at a 'final solution'.

Although few Jews are aware of the actual details of the appalling history of Jewish–Christian relations, all Jews have stored in their folk memory the knowledge that there has been a terrible past. The result is that among Orthodox Jews there is a period of mourning (like mourning for the dead) when a member of the family is baptized, so great is the feeling. (Fortunately this did not happen in my case.) A person who marries a Gentile may also be cut off from the family, especially if it is a son (in Jewish culture Jewishness is derived from the mother). Although I remained in good relations with my parents after my conversion, I found I no longer had contact with my uncles and aunts and cousins, or with Jewish friends and the Jewish community generally for many many years after I was baptized. Even my relations with my siblings were not easy. As an example of how Jews feel, when I was Bishop of Birmingham I was keen to bring the Holocaust Exhibition to the city, but the plan fell through because the rabbi was unwilling to sit on a committee with me.

Let me now consider some of the differences of belief between Judaism and Christianity. I do not mean that people who convert have to face up to these immediately. They probably do not even realize at the time that all these differences exist. But at some point they have to come to terms with them. In my case it has taken a good many years.

First and foremost there is the person and teaching of Jesus Christ. Consider first his teaching. While Christians admire it because it is so absolute and unconditional, Jews criticize it as utopian and unattainable. Certainly the track record of Christianity scarcely bears witness to a constant love of one's enemies, or going the extra mile, or not resisting evil. Rabbinic teaching, it is claimed, while similar in principle, is more down to earth, more within a person's grasp. Jewish critics say that we can control ourselves to the extent that we do not bear a grudge or seek revenge, but actually to love our enemies is quite beyond the powers of most of us, and Christians have abysmally failed to do this, at least so far as Jews are concerned. There is of course something to be said on both sides here, although I personally find the directness of the Sermon on the Mount both challenging and inspiring. There is a real different here. Judaism says 'Be good within your powers.' Christianity says 'Reach for impossible possibilities.'

More important than the teaching of Jesus is the person of Jesus. Orthodox Jews believe that the Messiah is still to come. Liberal Jews no longer pray for his coming, because they no longer believe in the Messiah, only the Messianic kingdom. Christians know that the Messiah has already come. 'Christ' is the Greek form for the Anointed One, which in Hebrew is *messiach* or Messiah. Unfortunately the word 'Christ' has now lost its original meaning, and is used as a kind of surname for Jesus.

Orthodox Jews believe that the role of the Messiah is to usher in the Messianic kingdom, in which the Jews will be vindicated. Their continuing discrimination at the hands of Christians and continuing anti-Semitism do not lead them to believe that the Messianic kingdom can have arrived: therefore Jesus could not have been the Messiah. The restoration of the kingdom of Israel, which was believed to accompany the Messiah, has been achieved not through the agency of the Messiah, but through force of arms. We may contrast this view with that of Christians, who believe that they are united to Christ through baptism, and that the Messiah has indeed inaugurated the Messianic kingdom; but Jesus the Messiah was different from what the Jews expected (so different that he never called himself the Messiah). Anyone changing from Judaism to Christianity changes his views about the Messiah.

It is not simply arguments about messiahship which divide Jews from Christians. There is a passage of Scripture which takes the place for Judaism that the Lord's Prayer holds for Christians. It is said several times a day. Its opening words are: 'Hear, O Israel: the

Lord our God, the Lord is one' (Deuteronomy 6.4 NIV). The unity of God is absolutely basic to Judaism as it is to Islam. Orthodox Jews regard Jesus as a false prophet, indeed, as *the* false prophet foretold in the Scriptures. Liberal Jews, as we have noted, do regard him as a true prophet. Both are united in denying that Jesus can in any sense be regarded as divine. 'How can a *man* possibly be divine?' they ask. But in the so called Nicene Creed Christians affirm that they believe in 'one Lord Jesus Christ, the only Son of God, God from God, Light from Light, begotten not made, of one being with the Father'. The subtleties of trinitarian doctrine are quite beyond Jews. They think that Christians are tritheists, that they believe in three Gods. Here is a large gap to be crossed in moving from the one faith to the other.

I have to admit (and this is probably due to my Jewishness) that I think that in one sense it is a pity that the Christian faith has been defined for all time in the Hellenistic categories which are used in the Nicene Creed from which I have just quoted. It was a necessary inculturation of the Christian faith at the time, and in that sense a good thing. But it means that the Christian faith must be defined in these metaphysical terms for all time, with the preincarnate Christ as 'of one being with the Father'. I doubt whether this metaphysical language is an adequate way in our contemporary culture of expressing the divine nature of Christ. I would prefer to speak of God embodied in human personality through the person of Jesus. Be that as it may, the Hellenistic way of thinking is certainly misleading for Jews. How could the person of Christ be adequately expressed in Hebrew terms? I am only speculating, but it might make use of the Hebrew word *shekinah* which expresses the immanent presence of God on earth. It might go like this: 'In Jesus the Messiah the *shekinah* dwelt fully during his lifetime so that through him we are in the presence of the Divine.' However, I realize that I am crying for the moon. The Church would never accept that, and Jews would interpret it in terms of their belief that Christians hold that there are three Gods.

The person of Jesus brings to light a difference in the interpretation of Scripture. Jews tend to hold the five books of Moses as the most important in the Bible, while for Christians pride of place is given to the prophets because they are believed to have foretold the Messiah. Jews refute this claim. They cannot see any foreshadowing in their Bible of the new covenant. How could they agree with the author of the Epistle to the Hebrews that the words of psalm 45.6 (RSV), 'Thy throne, O God, is for ever and ever', refer to the preincarnate Son of God, without having any prior belief in Jesus as Messiah? Orthodox Jews certainly looked on their Scriptures as containing prophecies of the Messiah – no less than 456 passages have been identified by rabbis as referring to him. But none are believed to refer to Jesus.

As an example, take Isaiah 53, with its prophecy of the Suffering Servant. Christians interpret the passage in two senses: first as referring to some contemporary or near-contemporary leader, and then, in a deeper meaning, as referring to the coming of Christ. Jewish sources also regard the passage as Messianic, but with a difference. The Hebrew 'he was smitten' becomes 'though we were accounted smitten' in the Aramaic paraphrase of the first century. Later the Jews interpreted the passage as referring to the Jewish nation as a whole. After much suffering at the hands of Gentiles, Jews would be rewarded with resurrection by God. Some interpretations could even accept that there would be a suffering Messiah, but never the kind of suffering endured by such an ignominious death as crucifixion. That would be unthinkable for a Jew. Here again there is a leap to be made between Judaism and Christianity.

This leads to the centrality of the cross for Christians. They believe that Christ suffered this cruel kind of death 'for us men and for our salvation'. The idea of Jesus' death as a sacrifice for sins is abhorrent to Jews. While martyrs might, as they saw it, make some kind of vicarious expiation, the Messiah could not possibly give his life as a self-sacrifice. His coming was to be a triumph, not a worldly disaster. In any case, the Day of Atonement was instituted for the forgiveness of sins. According to the Old Testament, this was the day when the High Priest went alone into the Holy of Holies in the temple. One goat was sacrificed as a sin offering, and the High Priest, after laying his hands on a second goat, sent it off into the wilderness bearing the sins of the people. After the Romans levelled the Jewish temple in AD 70, sacrifices could no longer be offered. In the Psalms it is written that God accepts the prayers of the heart rather than the blood of goats; and so today prayers are offered throughout the Day of Atonement; no work is done, a fast is kept and prayers of penitence are said. Jews believe that all that is needed for a right relationship with God is penitence and faith and a life consonant with these. But Christians believe that something deeper is needed. Before they can truly change their way, they need to be in a right relationship with God: they need to know that they have been accepted by a loving Father despite their wrongdoing, and it is through the death and resurrection of Christ that they know they have been forgiven, accepted and put into a right relationship with God. Here is another important difference between Judaism and Christianity.

This leads to other differences. Take the Holocaust: for Jews this is a terrible problem. How could God allow the genocide of his chosen people? It could not be a visitation of divine wrath on the Jews for not keeping the Law of Moses, for it was applied indiscriminately to all. Various explanations were given. Perhaps God gives people freedom to do what they like – but this does not exonerate God from his responsibility. Perhaps God is not omnipotent, jut indifferent. Perhaps there was an interruption of divine providence, as though God's attention was elsewhere. Perhaps there is no God. All these explanations have been put forward. Speaking as a Jewish Christian, I see it rather differently. If God's Messiah had to die a terrible and utterly undeserved death by crucifixion, this same terrible fate might also be ordained for God's chosen people. It does not make it any less terrible, but it does somehow account for the fact that the Jews have been treated down the ages so grossly unfairly, and yet have been resurrected to new life again and again. But I must not push this explanation. One distinguished rabbi has warned against Christianity pressing Judaism into its own construct.

Mention of the Holocaust – or the *Shoah*, as the Jews call it – leads to another difference. Jews cannot forgive those who carried out the Holocaust. They believe that forgiveness can only be given by God to the persons concerned; and since the perpetrators by now have almost all died, only God can forgive them, not the Jews themselves. By contrast there are the words in the Lord's Prayer: 'Forgive us our trespasses, as we forgive them that trespass againt us.'

These are the main differences in belief in making a transition from one faith to the other. There are differences too in worship. There are no sacraments in Judaism; but sacramental worship prevails in Christianity. The resemblances between baptism and circumcision are only superficial. The latter obviously applies to males only, and there is no sense in which it is sacramental: it is simply a sign of belonging to the covenant with Abraham. Again, *barmitzvah* is not a sacrament like confirmation (if that is indeed a sacrament): it is an occasion when a Jew takes upon himself his adult duties under the Law. Bread and wine used at the sanctification of the Sabbath in Judaism are not sacramental: these are blessed and eaten simply as a sign of God's bounty.

Christian worship, although it should be offered in the Spirit through Christ to the Father, is in fact usually Christ-centred, while Jewish worship is God-centred. Jewish worship is much more informal: Jews may well speak to one another during prayers, and at a wedding, instead of the Anglican silent hush before the arrival of the bride, Jews walk around and greet friends. Again, Christians are happy to speak direct to God. For Jews God is so holy that he may never be called by his name – Jehovah – but as *Adonai*, the Lord. It is noteworthy that the spirit of thanksgiving permeates all Jewish worship, which it certainly does not do, alas, in Christian worship. Here is just one example:

> Were our mouths filled with sacred song as the sea is with water, our tongues shouting loudly as the roaring billows, our lips with praise as the widely spread firmament, our eyes sparkling like the sun or moon, our hands spread out as the eagle's wings in the skies, and our feet as swift as the hind's; we should yet be unable to thank Thee sufficiently, O Lord our God! or adequately bless thy name, O our King! for even one of the many thousands and thousands of benefits that Thou hast vouchsafed to us and to our ancestors . . .

As for ethics, I have already mentioned that these stem from the same source, the two 'great commandments'. Judaism (at any rate in its orthodox form) is concerned with keeping the 248 positive and 368 negative commandments of the Mosaic Law (which include both moral, dietary and ritual commands). Christians often regard these as legalistic, but to a devout Jew the keeping of the Law is not just a duty but a joy, for it means doing the will of God. All religions, of course, can lapse into legalism. There are denominations of Christianity which are as legalistic (and sometimes more so) than orthodox Judaism. The commandments of the Torah were given long ago; they need interpreting and bringing up to date. This is the task of the Mishnah, and later the Talmud, which are given as great authority in Judaism as the Torah (rather as Roman Catholicism gives equal authority to Scripture and tradition). Further interpretation is needed to bring the Law up to date today. That is the task of the Jewish rabbi, to interpret Law, in contrast to the Christian priest, whose task is to pastor people and to nourish them with word and sacrament. When a Jew becomes baptized, there is a change of lifestyle. My own family did not keep the rabbinic law: they were content simply to obey the Law of Moses. Nonetheless there was a marked change in my lifestyle when I became a Christian, although I remember that when I first had bacon for breakfast it tasted like ashes in my mouth!

Naturally there are some differences in ethical traditions between the two faiths. The greatest is the doctrine of grace. Jews are expected, like Pelagians, to pull themselves up by their own bootstraps; in the Christian tradition we can only do this by God's grace – 'we can do no good thing without thee'. Jews, I think, are stronger on social ethics, beginning in the Old Testament. It is no coincidence that the Chief Rabbi is one of the foremost exponents of social ethics in this country. Differences over sexual matters are similar in Judaism and in Christianity. However, a Jewish woman cannot divorce her husband, but she can actually ask to be divorced if he does not give her sexual satisfaction. Again, the Sabbath is a time for joy, and for that reason Jewish husbands should make love to their wives on the Sabbath. In my wildest dreams I cannot envisage a Christian pastor exhorting his married flock to do that! Judaism is more down to earth about sex than Christianity. Not all converts to Christianity welcome its more restrictive attitudes.

There are other differences. Church services form the focus of Christian worship. In Judaism it is the home, and a father acts as a kind of priest to his family. Of course the holy day is Saturday, not Sunday. The Christian year is mostly Christ-centred, but in Judaism many of the feasts commemorate past deliverances of the Jews. Christians tend to be evangelistic; Jews are not. It is possible for a Gentile to become a Jew, but it is not easy.

I have spoken of differences in belief in changing from one religion to the other. But the main difference is belonging to another group. To change from one religion to another is to change one's membership to another fellowship with a different ethos. Judaism is primarily concerned with orthopraxy (doing the right thing), Christianity with orthodoxy (believing the right thing). Judaism is primarily a racial religion. It does not encourage proselytes; but Christianity is a universal faith or it is nothing. This difference is really important, and it has an important corollary. Jews were promised by God for all time the land of Israel. As a matter of fact, from 586 BC, when the Jews were deported to Babylon, until fifty years ago, when they declared independence for Israel, the Jews over all those centuries were only in charge of the government of the land of Israel for a mere 66 years, between the Maccabean revolt and the entry of the Roman general Pompey into the Jewish temple. For thousands of years – this was even the case in New Testament times – more Jews lived outside Israel than within it. Nonetheless it was the land which God promised to them. As a Jew I still feel glad that the Jews have regained sovereignty of the land given to their forefathers, although as a Christian I am appalled at the way in which Jews in Israel treat Arabs as second- or third-class citizens or worse. I find the situation so tragic that I am determined never to go back there, much as I draw inspiration from Jesus' Galilee and from Jerusalem where he was crucified and was raised from the dead.

There is one more issue to be explored. To become a Christian involves joining the Christian Church. In the Christian way of life, despite the official emphasis on orthodoxy, belonging is as impor-

tant as believing. But, sadly, as we all know, Christendom is badly
divided. Well, that is no new thing to a Jew, because Judaism also
is badly divided, with ultra-orthodoxy (usually small immigrant
Polish or Russian congregations), orthodoxy (represented by the
United Synagogue in Britain), Masorti Jews (who are pretty orthodox in practice, but who do not believe that Moses could have
written the first five books of the Bible as they now stand), Reformed
Jews (who worship in their vernacular tongue, but who are fairly
orthodox in practice), and Liberal and Progressive Jews (some of
whom are 'way out', sit light to dietary laws, and some of them
even question circumcision for their children). There are rough par-
allels here with Christian churches. One might, in a flight of fancy,
pair off the ultra-orthodox with the Eastern Orthodox Churches,
the Orthodox with the Roman Catholic Church, Masorti with An-
glicanism, Reformed with the Churches of the Reformation, and
Liberals – well there are liberals and ultra liberals in most Christian
churches.

The question arises: when a convert from Judaism joins the Christian Church, which Christian denomination does he or she join? On
that question I can give no advice. When I was being prepared for
baptism over sixty years ago, the minister who was preparing me
said 'I suppose you will join the Church of England?' and I said I
supposed I would; and I did. I simply wanted to be an ordinary
Christian, and so I joined the church of the land, because in those
days most people had some kind of connection, however tenuous,
with the Church of England, the established church of the country.
In fact I am glad that it has turned out that way, because although
there are times when the Church of England is perfectly infuriating,
I love it dearly, and now I could join no other. But I do not feel
able to give any general advice on this matter.

Note

1   A more detailed description can be found in my *On Being a Jewish Chris-
    tian* (Hodder, 1998), of which this lecture generally is a precis.

Chapter Three

OUT OF THE PLAYPEN

Anne Townsend

Questions have bothered me. Questions which do not allow themselves to be neatly shelved, or ignored for very long, for their property is such that they burrow and wriggle around in the deep recesses of my mind. When I dare to presume that they have disappeared for good, then they resurface to nag me afresh. They are questions like, 'How, and why, did I ever get *into* the fundamentalist end of evangelicalism in the first place in my early teens?' And, 'Whatever possessed me that in late mid life I landed myself, more or less, *outside* the culture and belief-system which, up till then, had comprised my whole life and *raison d'être*?'

Trying to find answers to my questions led me, in late mid life, first to study theology and later psychology. I suspect that I embarked on these lines of study with an unconscious hope that either the one, or the other, would supply me with *all* possible solutions and a complete answer. This has not been the case. Both have given me invaluable insights but only partial answers. Each has supplied clues which now lead me, like a detective or archaeologist, to attempt to piece together the fragments of discovered insights and to try to reconstruct something which makes sense. Some kind of shape is slowly emerging as I gradually see more clearly some of the crucial factors in my past which shaped the person I now am, and the person I once was. These factors include the type of family culture in which I was reared during the Second World War, the particular personalities of each of my parents, and my own personality – shaped by environment, by genetic inheritance, and also by those unconscious factors and fantasies which have been passed down the generations of my family.

At one time, I assumed that my religious beliefs had sprung simply from my subscribing to a certain theological outlook and a certain type of thinking. But I now understand that my particular brand of religion fitted in very well with my particular personality. It conveniently reinforced some of the psychological defence mechanisms (Klein 1993) which I commonly use both to keep myself going, to blind me to painful realities, and to twist harsh truth into something more palatable. The kind of God in which I believed also met certain of my internal psychological needs. In evangelicalism I had a good heavenly Father, who understood me perfectly and who loved me provided that I was 'good', and who could be trusted to meet all my needs generously and keep me safe from any harm. My fundamentalist outlook suited me well; it kept me safe and relatively comfortable, and fitted in with some of the basic premises of life in my family – premises that life was about always doing my very best and was also about unselfishly serving God and others. The snag was that in order to fit into this fundamentalist culture, I had to bridle my capacity to think and to question which had been such a vital part of life in my family. It was as if I were keeping myself as a toddler – one who plays contentedly in her playpen without risking exploration of the world beyond the safe confinement and containment of her pen. This lasted until internal and external events tossed me out of the playpen and into –? What, I knew not! It was far too fearful at first even to try to understand what was happening to me (Townsend 1996).

One of the people who helped me in my early struggles to understand myself and what had happened to me was the Cambridge theologian Professor James Barr, who in his student days had belonged to a zealous, Christian fundamentalist student organization. He has written extensively and influentially about Christian fundamentalism in more than one book. When I first came across his writings and later went to talk to him, it was a great relief to discover that I was not alone in my struggles, and to realize that others had similar difficulty and fears in changing from this form of faith into something different. James Barr articulated my experience before I had found words of my own to express what it was like for me. He writes:

> Many ... who enter the Christian faith enter it through the gateway of fundamentalism ... many who do so, come to feel after some time that it is a truly inadequate form of the Christian religion. The finding of a way out, however, is no easy undertaking. The transition to a different understanding of the Bible, of faith, and of the church can be a time of deep uncertainty and often of severe personal suffering. Fundamentalist society will do little or nothing to help the pilgrim who becomes convinced that he must leave it and seek a different world of faith ... (Barr 1984, p. vii)

And in a revision of an earlier book on the same subject, he explains that

perhaps the most uncertain point in the whole matter is the
question of the psychological explanation of fundamentalism . . .
My reason for avoiding [this] . . . was, first of all, a reluctance to
accept that any doctrinal position could be explained simply as a
consequence of psychological conditions; and secondly, the observation that those who experience an evangelical conversion are
often free and open people, both in themselves and in the first
stages after their conversion, and that it is the increasing involvement in fundamentalist doctrine and the life of a fundamentalist
society that produces the marked psychological characteristics
which some have noted. Thus, I have thought that the people
concerned were not inherently this way; rather, fundamentalist
doctrine and life made them so . . . however, lacking as I do any
deep knowledge of psychology, I feel I have to hesitate in this . . .
(Barr 1981, p. xi)

I have thought a lot about the question he raises as to whether it is
the structure of fundamentalism itself which *initially* is responsible
for shaping adherents in a particular manner, or whether it is
people with certain personality structures or traits who are drawn
into fundamentalist churches. I find myself increasingly drawn to
conclude that it is precisely *because* of certain personality structures,
deficits and needs that a high proportion of people (of course, not
all) who now are, or who have been, Christian fundamentalists initially moved into such a church. I think that this is what happened
both in my own case and also in that of certain people with whom
my work as a priest and as a psychotherapist brings me into
contact. As I see it, some people are *unconsciously* drawn into Christian fundamentalism because of what they believe is on offer both
in the religious belief-system and also in the authoritarian, paterna-
listic, warm family-like church structures, in the conscious or unconscious hope that they will discover something which they
require, or make up for something lacking in themselves, or find
healing or wholeness.

So, how was it that I was attracted into this form of Christianity,
and what were some of the factors which many years later moved
me away from it? My minds goes back to a Saturday afternoon in
January, just over twenty years ago. By this stage in my life, my
hold on the clear-cut, secure beliefs of my evangelicalism were
already shaky. A phone call that afternoon knocked me for six –
and nothing has been the same since. I heard that afternoon that
seven of my friends (three of them mothers who were expecting to
deliver their babies within weeks) and five of their pre-school children had all been killed simultaneously in a terrible road accident

in Thailand, where we had (up till then) been working together as medical missionaries.

This awful event seared, scarred, melted and moulded me in the deepest recesses of my innermost being. It changed me considerably both spiritually and emotionally. My unconscious assumption at the time of the accident had been that the horror of this happening was charged with power to destroy me. Indeed, in the immediate period of months after the blow, I felt as if I were falling apart with no one and nothing to hold and contain all the chaotic fragments of that which was myself. Like Humpty-Dumpty, I had fallen off my wall and was convinced that even 'all the king's horses and all the king's men, couldn't put Humpty together again'. To my amazement, I realize years later that the enormity of my loss was not as personally destructive as it had seemed at the time, but rather it became the crucial factor which strengthened and deepened not only my faith but also the quality of the person I am in the process of becoming. This terrible event catapulted me, once and for all, out of my playpen. Illusion was shattered and I had to try to face reality. This was a significant milestone on a journey which was leading me in search of my hidden, real self – as opposed to the compliant external 'Me' (Klein 1993) which I had constructed down the years to fit in comfortably with the expectations of my family and later of evangelical culture.

As a young teenager, I had joyfully embraced Jesus Christ as Lord and Saviour. It was as if I had responded to a clarion call to 'get on board the glory train', and words to the effect that 'you must hurry to get your ticket tonight or you might miss your chance of eternal salvation for ever!' And so, when the whistle blew at 9.15 p.m. precisely, from a platform in Eastbourne Town Hall, one August evening, at a 'Youth for Christ' evangelistic rally, I joined the ranks of eager 'enquirers' clambering on board this particular religious 'train'. I travelled on it for many years with zeal, dedication and enthusiasm. It was 'all or nothing for God' as far as I was concerned. As I understood it, this was the one and only route to the destination called 'eternal salvation' and I was warned that should I abandon the train there might be no future way of reaching its heavenly destination. Bible words were quoted about the terrifying lostness of those who 'turn their backs on so great a salvation' and of the fearful fate of those who, once 'having tasted the gospel', then question it. Put crudely, I understood the teaching to state that once you were on this train, you must never get off, for leaving the train meant that your destination after life could only be one place – hell, which spelled terrifying eternal damnation, punishment, lostness and abandonment.

The form of evangelicalism which gripped me and ruled my existence from that time onwards was something relatively simple. As I saw it (possibly mistakenly), it called for much blind faith and little serious grappling with theological mysteries. Matters religious were either clearly black or white, right or wrong, of God or of the devil. Mystery, paradox and doubt were not ingredients of this form of faith. I did what I thought was expected of me by God, and in turn expected God to take care of me and mine. I did my best to accept that the Bible was the infallible, inspired and authoritative Word of God, to be taken very seriously, not to be questioned, and to be used as the basis from which my daily living would spring. I am aware that to call such religious beliefs 'evangelical Christianity' does injustice to those many evangelicals who have grappled with complex issues, who have understood that mystery like the ultimate Mystery which is God cannot be solved as one can solve a detective story, and who have found ways of holding the tensions engendered in paradox in their fragile spiritual hands. I was not acquainted with evangelicals who attempted to do this.

My belief-system (which I, and others, called 'evangelical') was one in which for years I suspended, in a selective manner, my capacity for reasoned thought. The exception to this was any line of reasoning which allowed me to master certain lines of thought which led to and reinforced those conclusions which were already part and parcel of the package I regarded as fundamental to my faith. I tended to know what I reckoned the Bible 'ought to' say and what I thought God 'ought to' be like, and then used my mind to 'prove' that this was so. An enthusiastic reader of the Bible, I developed a capacity for overlooking and ignoring those parts of the Bible which disagreed with my ideas of what the Bible 'ought to' be saying about God or life in general. I managed to turn a blind eye to Old Testament concepts of a God who not only was good, just and merciful but also appeared at times to be harsh, intolerant, cruel and unjust. In retrospect, it is hard for me to understand how I managed to do this, for there was nothing wrong with my brain – on the contrary, at school I won scholarships and at medical school distinctions and prizes. I had managed unconsciously to split off a certain reasoning aspect of my personality from my mind and to separate it from my religious self. It took a terrible road accident finally to shake me, wake me, and set me off thinking through all kinds of unorthodox things which I had assumed would land me up in hell. As a doctor I could question, search and reason and yet, when it came to the 'Christian me', I had handicapped myself so that my reasoning faculties malfunctioned.

My journey still is disturbing and painful. A year after that traumatic accident, and after sixteen years of medical missionary work in Thailand, we returned as a family to England and I chose to work for leading evangelical organizations. As the author of a number of popular religious books, I was well known and in demand as a public speaker. I did as I always did – I did what others expected of me and what I expected of myself. My outer façade was still just present but it was precarious, with its ever-widening cracks covered by very thin tissue. Worrying implications connected with the deaths of my friends gnawed relentlessly within me. How could I believe in the kind of God I was proclaiming from platforms (one who cared especially for those of us who were his special 'born-again' ones – i.e. evangelical Christians – and who would never allow us to be harmed) when God had not prevented the terrible accident which killed my friends? Even more upsetting were the words of some who declared that God had permitted the accident 'for his greater glory'. The basis of my faith was increasingly shaky and I was increasingly aware of the hypocrisy involved when I addressed religious gatherings. My children were now in their teens and my family life was not at all as I liked to make it out to be on those occasions when I was perched high on a pedestal giving the appearance of being an example of 'successful Christianity'. I was frightened that our fragile family unit could no longer stand the pressures bursting out from inside, and crushing inwards from outside it. My husband, who now worked for a Third World relief agency, was frequently abroad on business and I felt isolated and increasingly helpless in all that was happening within and without.

In mid life, I was forced to recognize that being a 'full-time Christian worker' had not imparted the trouble-free existence I had assumed was guaranteed to missionaries and 'full-time Christian workers' such as me. I was forced to start to look under the shell of the self which I saw in my mirror and to explore secret inner parts of myself, to grapple with many of the questions and to face some of the doubts which I had banished or buried most of my life. Perhaps I had hoped that if I ignored them they would go away, but this was not to be. They erupted, revealing all the shameful mess concealed for so many years. I was also forced to notice that my kind of Christians were not as completely 'good, pure, and holy' as I had thought we all were. I saw with clarity something I had missed out on before – that even we ('God's elect and chosen ones') had a dark, Shadow-side to our personalities. Being 'born again' and being 'sanctified' had not painted me with God's internal white-wash or bleached me whiter than white inside. I could no longer project (Klein 1993) everything nasty onto the devil or onto things and onto people outside myself and my church. I found all sorts of 'nastiness' lurking within myself and to my great surprise discovered that they imparted their own brand of strength when owned and integrated as part of myself. Illusions about myself as an evangelical Christian, about the evangelical culture of that time, and about the God of that brand of evangelicalism were being shattered – leaving me in emotional, pychological, spiritual and theological disarray.

My dictionary defines the word 'illusion' as being 'a perception that is not true to reality, having been altered subjectively in the mind of the perceiver'. Psychologists of various schools have pondered on the subject of illusion and how and why it is present to a greater or lesser degree in most (if not all) of us. It is a necessary part of infant life, and persists to some degree in the adult (Rizzuto 1979). When an adult, like me, constructs his or her life around (what arguably could be termed) an illusion, then vital questions must be asked – disconcerting questions like: 'If illusion serves one or more intrapsychic purposes, then what might they be?' and 'Why is this particular illusion necessary for this particular individual?'

Illusions, according to Sigmund Freud, the founding father of psychoanalysis, are 'not necessarily false'. But rather, he states that he calls 'a belief an illusion when wish-fulfilment is a prominent factor' (Freud 1927). Following Freud's thinking, I might, therefore, postulate that because I wanted to have an all-powerful, all-providing father for all of my life, I therefore unconsciously 'dreamed up' just such a father in my particular concept of God.

According to Freud's particular perception, religion performs three functions. First, he regards civilization as being a source of human misery because it imposes controls on instincts. The forces of civilization usually are strong enough to prevent people from following basic instincts to their limits. Although the adult, mature, rational person accepts this, the immature (and, according to Freud, therefore the 'childlike' person) may demand or require an ultimate reward in the heavenly realm of eternal bliss. In other words, this line of thought might go something like this: 'I can't have everything I need to satisfy all my requirements, my desires, and my cravings in this life. But never mind, I'll have more than this in heaven and so I can carry on in this life relatively contented, knowing great bliss will be mine later on.' This can be regarded as a version of 'pie in the sky when you die'.

Second, Freud points out, nature is impersonal, mechanical and uncaring. His mature, adult person is the person who is able to accept this state of affairs and to live with the harsh reality that life is meaningless and purposeless. On the other hand, his immature person acts like an infant and flees from such reality into the illusion of there being a caring, providential God who stands behind nature's impersonal façade. In other words, a way of applying this might be to adopt an attitude of: 'My life only makes sense and has meaning if I can think of an omnipotent, all-loving God who always, in all situations, works out his *good* purposes in my life – both in the hard and in the easy times. I, therefore, trust that he has a plan for my personal welfare and well-being and this makes me feel secure and helps me through the tough times ... sometimes I even feel like a baby safe and comforted in its mother's arms ...'

Third, according to Freud, fate continually deals out harsh blows to human grandiosity – the greatest being death. It is not easy for us humans to accept our limitations and vulnerability. Freud's mature, adult rational person accepts this; his grandiose and infantile person cannot agree that life is temporary and so clings to the illusion of life after death (Jones 1953). This might go something like this: 'I must personally be of value and importance for God to have sent his Son to die just for me, and for him then to have prepared a special place for me in heaven ...'

According to Freud, we are to develop from being people who are emotionally infantile and immature into adult rational maturity. We should not need these illusions to give us warm feelings of well-being. We ought to be able to see and handle reality rather than resort to psychological mechanisms enabling us to flee from painful reality. He teaches that a mature person has developed beyond the stage of requiring the illusion of religion to keep them going or to bolster them up.

Needless to say, his views have been widely explored and challenged by many people. Early on, in response to Freud's sending him his work entitled *The Future of an Illusion*, the French philosopher Romain Rolland agreed with Freud that religious belief might at times be an expression of childish needs. However, he asked Freud to consider religious *experience* separately from *belief*. In a religious context, *experience* seems to be equated with feelings and emotions, and *belief* with the thinking capacity of the mature mind. When he was in India, Rolland had himself experienced a blissful submersion into what he called 'the oceanic' – these are feelings which apparently parallel those of a baby merging contentedly with its mother at her breast. These experiences, he explained, should be distinguished from the illusion of religion because the latter induces infantile wish-fulfilment, but the former, he states, did not 'in any way harm my critical faculties and my freedom to exercise them'. In other words, he could experience this, while his rational and thinking *mind* continued to function as that of a mature adult.

The modern day Argentinian psychoanalyst Ana-Maria Rizzuto

(who now works in the USA) has studied and researched how people are likely to have come to have the religious beliefs which they have. She agrees with J. Jones when he states that

> the outstanding conclusion that emerges from all of this investigation is that the religious life represents a dramatisation on a cosmic plane of the emotions, fears and longings which arise in the child's relation to his parents. (Jones 1996)

Rizzuto and Jones follow a psychological model called 'object relations theory' which was developed from the groundwork which Freud had established. Object relations theory was started off by Melanie Klein, developed by other later workers, and is very influential in the UK counselling and psychotherapy arena today. A very simple way of looking at this would be to state that contained in everyone's mind are permanent fragments of that person's perception of how things were experienced and felt from their earliest infancy onwards. So, someone might contain perceptions of their own mother as usually being warm and loving, and of father as being distant and authoritative. These inner perceptions (which may or may not match actual external reality) are then projected outwards, onto certain receptive people, situations or 'things' outside the person's mind, which offer a screen (as in the cinema) onto which they can be projected (Klein 1993). Rizzuto and others suggest that this is one of the ways in which a child's understanding of God develops. The child projects onto the screen called 'God' that which mother, father and other significant people were perceived to be and the feelings associated with relationships to them. Over time, this is modified and God becomes either like what mother and father were for the child, or else God becomes a compensatory figure supplying what mother and father were *not* experienced to be. Over the years, usually this God-concept is further modified and altered.

Freud believed that people must grow out of any need for what he regarded as their 'illusion' of God, and learn to live with reality – no matter how harsh it is. Rizzuto had a different opinion from Freud. She writes: 'I must disagree. Reality and illusion are not contradictory terms. Psychic reality – whose depth Freud so brilliantly unveiled – cannot occur without that specifically human transitional space for play and illusion' (Rizzuto, 1979, p. 209).

When she speaks of the 'transitional space', Rizzuto is referring to work by the paediatrician Donald Winnicott, who taught that there is an area in the mind in which religion is able to develop – it is in this particular part of the mind that a child plays with ideas and is creative (Winnicott 1986). It is here that a child's teddy bear or 'cuddly' stands in for mother and conjures up feelings of her presence. The 'cuddly' creates the illusion of the presence of mother or the primary care-giver. Rizzuto continues:

> To ask a man to renounce a God he believes in may be as cruel and as meaningless as wrenching a child from his teddy bear so that he can grow up. We know nowadays that teddy bears are not toys for spoiled children but are part of the illusory substance of growing up. Each developmental stage has transitional objects appropriate for the age and level of maturity of the individual ... Asking a mature, functioning individual to renounce his God would be like asking Freud to renounce his own creation, psychoanalysis, and the 'illusory' promise of what scientific knowledge can do. Men cannot be men without illusions. The type of illusion we select – science, religion, or something else – reveals our personal history and the transitional space each of us has created between his objects and himself to find a 'resting place' to live in (Rizzuto 1979, p. 209)

In recent years, studying psychology has opened my eyes to some of the psychological possibilities about why as a teenager I was drawn into the form of evangelicalism to which I was attracted. But such thinking raises disturbing questions about the very existence of God – questions which the theologian Hans Küng tackles:

> And must God ... be merely a human wishful structure, an infantile illusion or even a purely neurotic delusion? As we have argued elsewhere ... a real God may certainly correspond to the wish for God ... It does not follow – as some theologians have mistakenly concluded – from man's profound desire for God and eternal life that God exists and eternal life and happiness are real. But those atheists who think that what follows is the non-existence of God and the unreality of eternal life are mistaken too. Here then we reach the crux of the problem, which is not at all difficult to understand and in the face of which any kind of projection theory, opium theory, or illusion theory momentarily loses its suggestive power. Perhaps this being of our longings and dreams does actually exist. Perhaps this being who promises us eternal bliss does exist. Not only the bliss of the baby at its mother's breast ... but a quite different reality in the future which corresponds to the unconscious and conscious aspirations precisely of the mature adult human being and to which the oldest, strongest, most urgent wishes of mankind are oriented, which can fulfil our longings for infinite happiness. Perhaps. Who knows? (Küng 1990, pp. 78–80)

In the early stages of my struggles simply to survive what was happening to me, and later on as I tried to make sense of it within a theological and psychological perspective, I felt very isolated. The time came when I mustered up enough courage to go public on television, radio and through books and articles to share what had happened to me with people in that segment of evangelical Christian culture who knew of me from my previous writings. I began to discover not just scores of others like me, but thousands of us. Many people wrote to me to thank me for expressing through my story an experience which paralleled theirs. In the last ten or so years, I have received hundreds of such letters, and continue to receive them.

The story I had to tell was of initially chaotic, disturbing, terrifying but ultimately life-enhancing internal changes that had taken place inside me. I was no longer the person others still assumed me to be. I sensed that I needed to set the record right and to be as honest as I dared. But I knew that I would face criticism and longed to go on being loved and accepted by those people (some known to me and others unknown) who most of my life had been my 'church family'. I risked ostracism and that was costly. I also had to come to terms with the guilt I felt for 'defecting' from the faith I had once shared with these others. Some of them would empathize with my predicament, but I also realized that I was cutting myself off from any of those whose capacity to understand was so limited that they would now be unable to accept me and might humiliatingly treat me as a 'backslider to be won back to the fold'.

I also had a sense of guilt and that I was deserting 'the one and only true faith' – which to me was my brand of fundamentalist evangelicalism. I suspect that, unless you have been involved in this type of church culture, you may well be amazed that a professional woman like me could be so afraid. But, along with others like me, that's how it was for me.

In the past, from time to time, I had tried to share my despair and my crumbling beliefs with fellow evangelical Christian leaders. Only one clergyman of my religious ilk made determined efforts to understand, but he lived a long way away from me and so I was unable to spend much time with him. I spent a day at his home while he gently listened to my story and prayed for me. The others to whom I talked gave me the impression that if only I prayed harder, read my Bible more, 'claimed God's promises', had a prolonged holiday, or took a sabbatical, everything would be all right. But it wasn't. With hindsight, those pastors have my sympathy. How do you help someone, like me, who has always tended to be the one to whom clergy turn for help and who doesn't know how to ask for herself? My doctor called me 'the smiling Mona Lisa' and I realize that most of the time I masked my spiritual and emotional agony so effectively that it was well covered with make-up and bright lipstick. This was part of my philosophy that 'witnessing Christians' were supposed to look happy and well in order to be a good advertisement and thus to 'lead others to Christ'! Hardly surprising that no one came alongside to help. The worst pain was that of feeling abandoned by the God in whose service I had spent my life.

Confronted with some of the harsh realities about myself, I felt so isolated and helpless that the only way I could see out of the horror of my despair was to end my life. But my unplanned and unsuccessful attempt to bring about an ending turned into a new beginning. After my suicide attempt, the curate and two senior women from my evangelical church came and spent time with me daily for several weeks. But then they moved to other pressing pastoral concerns. My psychiatrist acquiesced in my request for as many pills as I could safely consume to deaden the pain and so my turbulent emotions were splinted and dulled. No one suggested I should see a counsellor or therapist to try to get to the root of the problem.

It was after that that I landed up in the office of a senior hospital chaplain. As far as I was concerned there was no way in which he could even be counted as being a Christian! He was not one of those who had been 'soundly converted' according to the way in which I thought 'sound conversions' took place. He asked penetrating and disconcerting questions about the Bible which I had tried very hard to convince myself was word for word inspired by God and could, therefore, never be questioned. He didn't seem to believe in an afterlife containing flames from hell – from which I had spent much of my life preaching and teaching that people must be saved. Not only was he a trained psychotherapist, but his tutor during his theological training had been none other than David Jenkins, the former outspoken Bishop of Durham. My restricted religious viewpoint suggested that 'if you let a psychotherapist into your brain then you let in the devil and all his evil works'. It also suggested that there was some kind of affinity between the dreaded Antichrist and said bishop! This hospital chaplain was the last person I would have imagined could help me, for his theological stance was one which (according to that which I had gleaned down the years) could lead only to sure and everlasting destruction. Together he and I talked, week in and week out. He allowed me to do what my fundamentalism had forbidden and to struggle with doubts in such a way that they led not to death but became the seeds from which new ways of being and believing were conceived.

With his support I started off on what has led to recent past years of theological and psychological exploration and all sorts of discoveries. This became possible when I discovered that I could live with uncertainty and did not have to have a faith which was watertight in order to survive spiritually. I began to develop what John Keats, in his letters to George and Thomas Keats in 1817, called 'negative capability'. He explains: 'Negative Capability, that is, when a man is capable of being in uncertainties, mysteries, doubts, without any irritable reaching after fact and reason.'

I now realize from many people who have contacted me in recent years that I am but one of thousands of former evangelical Christians from the more fundamentalist end of evangelicalism who have discovered the terror, isolation and guilt of moving away from their familiar religious pathways to experience the thrill of journeying through new territory – through spiritual 'channel tunnels', in space-ships and hang-gliders, foot-slogging in barren deserts and lush, formerly forbidden, green pastures. As I have now attained three score years, I am grateful that my journey has been the one it has been. I am glad to have left the spiritual 'playpen' in which I barricaded myself away for a large part of my life.

References and Further Reading

Barr, J. ([1977] 1981), *Fundamentalism*, revised edition, London: SCM Press.

Barr, J. (1984), *Escaping from Fundamentalism*, London: SCM Press.

Freud, S. (1927), *The Future of an Illusion*, Standard Edition Vol. 21, London: Hogarth Press.

Jones, J. (1996), *Religion and Psychology in Transition*, New Haven, CT: Yale University Press.

Klein, J. (1993), *Our Need for Others and Its Roots in Infancy*, London: Routledge.

Küng, H. (1990), *Freud and the Problem of God*, New Haven, CT: Yale University Press.

Rizzuto, A.-M. (1979), *The Birth of the Living God*, Chicago, IL: University of Chicago Press.

Townsend, A. (1996), *Good Enough for God*, London: SPCK.

Winnicott, D. (1986), *Playing and Reality*, Harmondsworth: Penguin Books.

Chapter Four

BRINGING THEM IN:
Some Observations on Methods of Recruitment Employed by New Religious Movements

Eileen Barker

The first, and one of the most important things that must be said about the new religions is that they differ enormously from each other in a number of ways, including the ways in which they try to gain new recruits. The movements may be more or less (or not at all) actively involved in the task of recruitment; some may be trying to bring about conversions only, others may also be trying to secure a commitment from their converts to dedicate their lives to the movement (by living in special centres and/or working full time for the movement); the methods they use in their mission work may involve exerting more or less pressure on the potential recruit – and so on. In this paper I shall make no attempt to describe the full range of recruitment practices of the new religions, but, after a very short introduction, I shall try to suggest some of the ways in which the methods of recruitment of the new religions might be *approached*. In doing this, I shall be raising some rather obvious points, which do, despite their obviousness, frequently get forgotten, but which it might be helpful to keep in mind in our discussions.

The Environment

It is, of course, obvious that recruitment does not (cannot) take place in a social vacuum. There have been situations in which a particular truth is assumed to be so self-evidently The Truth that no one even thinks of questioning it – any more than one would think of questioning the fact that night will fall and be followed by another day. Muslim (or Catholic) parents living in an exclusively Muslim (or Catholic) environment would be extremely unlikely even to consider whether or not they ought to bring up their child in the Muslim (or Catholic) faith. We might wish to note that in such a society 'mission' is unnoticed, but, sociologically at least, it could be said that an exceptionally efficient method is being employed.

In a social environment in which there is more than one religious option available, there might be a 'live and let live' philosophy in which those of different faiths accept that 'many are the ways'; alternatively, there might be strong divisions, with each side convinced that they alone hold the truth and that people on the other side are not only wrong, but ought to be shown to be wrong and, by one means or another, brought to their senses. In the contemporary West, there are numerous societies that enjoy both religious pluralism and a political democracy that is dedicated to the principle of freedom of belief for all citizens. In some of these societies (in England and in Scandinavia, for example), there is an established church; in other countries, although there is no establishment, there are long-established ties with a particular religion (such as the Catholic Church) and/or political parties strongly associated with a Christian denomination; in some countries proselytizing is or has until recently been forbidden (as in the case of several non-western societies and much of Eastern Europe); in other countries (such as the United States) the Constitution demands that there be no inference into or promotion of religious beliefs on the part of the state. There are, in short, a number of different social environments within which new (or old) religions have more or less freedom to try to convert others to their faith.

The openness of the social environment to proselytizing endeavours will have some effect on the numbers of ways that a movement will make the first contact with potential recruits – and the kind of response that missionary activities will receive. In California, one can see posters on every street corner advertising meetings or phone numbers that will lead us to some new truth (I was once offered six different truths in the course of one crossing of San Francisco's Union Square); in several Arab countries and the former Soviet Union, Unificationists and International Society for Krishna Consciousness (ISKCON) devotees have been imprisoned for speaking their faith (as have Jehovah's Witnesses, Baptists, Catholics and others).

A Variety of Methods

Other things being equal (which, of course, they seldom are), movements that are offering obviously religious beliefs and/or ways of life are likely to focus on making personal contacts – either in a public place, or by knocking on people's doors or, quite commonly, through previously existing networks of friends and relations; while movements that are seeking to sell courses in self-enlightenment and/or self-development are more likely to advertise impersonally. This is not, however, an invariable rule. The Landmark Forum relies almost exclusively on word of mouth to attract new guests to its seminars and the Unification Church has frequently looked for new members through posters and small ads – although with very little success.

Again, speaking very generally, the self-development/spiritual-fulfilment types of movements (Scientology, Transcendental Meditation, the School of Economic Science) are likely to offer 'guests' (or 'clients') a series of meetings, seminars, classes or courses, the first one of which may be free or available for a token fee. The guest, having obtained a flavour of the group's beliefs and/or practices, may then be prevailed upon to proceed to further levels – each level frequently involving not only more of the person's money, but also more of his or her time and commitment. Movements (such as ISKCON or the Unification Church in their early days) that are looking for a religious commitment to a communal way of life, in which it is people's full-time dedication (or, in rather crude economic terms, their earning-power rather than their earning) that is being sought, have been more likely to press the potential recruit to join the members for a residential visit (often referred to as a workshop or a seminar) in which they could not only learn about the movement's beliefs and aims, but also gain first-hand knowledge of the everyday life of the movement – although, not surprisingly, these residential introductions have rarely been held in 'normal' working centres, but in special places that are used exclusively or primarily for recruitment purposes. Several movements have offered both courses and a communal lifestyle.

The methods used by the various movements will differ to some degree according to what it is that the movement is trying to offer the potential recruit, but most movements will employ some sort of combination of carrots and sticks. There will be the promises of novel relations of, perhaps, ancient truths, of a deeper understanding of the way God, people and/or the cosmos work; promises of closer relationships with God, with one's fellow beings, and/or with one's innermost self; promises of playing a role in creating a new kingdom of heaven on earth, changing the world, setting up a utopian enclave; and/or promises of communicating with the deep mysteries of the beyond and/or the within. There will be warnings of lost opportunities, of opening oneself, or abandoning oneself (or the world) to dark forces and/or Satan, of not realizing one's full potential, not being truly free, but forever bound by the conventions or accretions of society, of letting down oneself, one's family, one's new friends, the world and/or God. Testimonials (in the form of letters from transformed and grateful customers or talks from bright-eyed 'born-again' members) tell of the wonderful changes that can take place in a person's life once they have accepted the new truth; and, at the same time, stories may be whispered of fearful happenings that have befallen those who were offered but rejected the opportunities given by the new truth.

Movements that employ techniques (such as chanting, meditation, yoga or 'auditing') are likely to give the prospective recruit an introduction to these at an early, if not the first, meeting. There is often an atmosphere of intense excitement or reassuring calm in introductory sessions. Those in charge may exude authority or love or, quite often, both. Often the guest will undergo some quite grilling questioning about his or her beliefs and aspirations, but however demanding such sessions may be they are usually experienced as exhilarating by the convert – they are, after all, focused on the individual, and he or she is unlikely to have been the subject of such interest on many other occasions. Sometimes the guest is invited/cajoled to 'let yourself go – completely'. This can appear quite a frightening 'method'. During an extremely intensive weekend with the Rajneeshee, I became very worried when one of my fellow-guests seemed to have lost control of himself and was screaming hysterically at a cushion with which he was bashing up an already battered mattress. 'That's beautiful, let it all come out,' cooed our instructor into a microphone. I was anxiously checking that the second-floor windows were firmly closed and the door to the roof barred when she continued: 'But don't forget that your saliva may be contaminated.' Whereupon a helper proffered a box of Kleenex to the apparently possessed guest, who obediently reached out a hand, took a tissue, wiped his mouth, and then continued with his hysteria. I relaxed.

Brainwashing Techniques?

Several of the movements have leaders who are labelled charismatic. I have, however, found little evidence that many members actually *joined* because of any Svengali-like powers of the leader. Furthermore, the movements tend to attract people on an individual basis – there are few reports of mass conversions as a result of revival-type evangelical meetings.

Despite the allegations that have been presented in the media and elsewhere, neither I nor any serious student of the better-known new religions has ever come across any use of *physical* coercion in recruitment practices. Some groups (possibly Synanon and certainly the People's Temple, the Manson family and the SLA) have prevented people from leaving their premises – but such instances do not fall under the heading of recruitment into the new religions.

But lack of physical coercion certainly does not mean that some other kind of coercion and/or deceptive methods may not be used.

The movement with which I have had the most contact is the Unification Church, about which it has often been said that it employs both deception and brainwashing in order to obtain its recruits. In 1981 a popular British tabloid, the *Daily Mail*, won a libel case that the Unification Church brought against it on account of an article that it had published in 1978, accusing the movement of brainwashing and breaking up families. It was partly because I was so disturbed by the evidence and deliberations that I heard in court during this case that I ended up by devoting a 300-page book to the question of whether or not the Moonies do, indeed, use brainwashing techniques.[1]

Let me make it clear, my concern was not because a court could decide that it was legitimate for a newspaper to accuse a new religious movement of brainwashing. I happen to believe that people *can* use unacceptable means of persuasion; and I happen to believe that if they do so then it is permissible – even desirable – for newspapers (academics or whomsoever) to reveal/expose such practices. But I also happen to believe that, on the one hand, religious beliefs cannot be judged as true or false by the courts – largely on the ground that, epistemologically, most of the claims they make are not susceptible to empirical testing and, thus, there is no way in which disagreements can be resolved. (Inconsistency is frequently celebrated as paradox in theological discourse.) *And*, on the other hand, I happen to believe that there are ways of judging the truth or falsity of statements about behaviour that *are* amenable to empirical (and logical) scrutiny.

What worried me in the *Daily Mail* case (and in innumerable other claims that Moonies are brainwashed) was the apparent disregard for these two positions: on the one hand, there was the implication that anyone who could believe the 'gobbledegook' of the Unification theology must be brainwashed – or mad – because it was 'so obviously wrong'; on the other hand, the methodology of the 'scientific expertise' called upon by the *Daily Mail* was about as unscientific as one could imagine.

There is no space to go into details concerning all the falsities (as I see them) that are invoked by those who claim that new religions employ brainwashing techniques, but I would like to address just a few of the most common.

At the most crude level, there is the purely tautological assertion that anyone who believes that sort of rubbish and/or who is prepared to live that sort of life *must* be brainwashed – otherwise, why would they believe and/or do such things? This, of course, is no more than an assertion posing as an explanation. A slightly more elaborate version of the tautology is that it would be impossible for a particular person to change in such a way because he or she was so different before the conversion. The problem with these sorts of 'explanations' is, as the Unificationists themselves continually complain, that there is no way in which they could prove that a genuine, voluntary conversion could have taken place. When the Unificationists protest that they have chosen to be members of their church, they are merely told that they have been brainwashed into believing that they had made a free choice. (It is, however, possible that members of the new religions will be convinced that something did happen to them which, in fact, they could not resist – but in such a case they are likely to insist that it was God, not other people, who did it.)

Arguments purporting to substantiate claims that brainwashing takes place frequently include both statements about the processes to which the potential recruit is subjected at the Unification workshops, and statements about the state the person was/is after he or she became a Moonie. In the first category (which concentrates on the process), one finds accusations of such things as hypnosis, sugar-buzzing and/or inadequate diet, sensory deprivation, sensory over-stimulation, an overly controlled environment, deception and 'love-bombing'. In the second category (which concentrates on the state of the convert), one hears of glassy-eyed robots with such characteristics as inability to concentrate, loss of interest in former friends, hobbies, career, etc., changed physical appearance, an uncritical passivity *and* a tendency to be hypercritical.

Now, *of course*, someone who has experienced a genuine conversion will change. St Paul was hardly the same man after his experience on the road to Damascus. It is possible to argue that *anyone* who converts or, to put it in more secular terms, radically changes his or her mind about the way things are, must have been brainwashed (had their mind changed) – or become definitely peculiar. I am assuming, however, that this is not a point at issue; that is, I am assuming that we can allow for the possibility of 'genuine' conversion. I am also assuming that those who accuse the new religions of using brainwashing tactics believe that free choice and genuine conversions are possible, as they are claiming that something which could be termed free will has been removed from the 'victim'.

But what do we mean by free will? How is it possible to determine whether or not it is being exercised? In particular, is there any way in which we can try to judge whether or not people who themselves assert that they are making freely chosen decisions are, in fact, mistaken? Is there any way out of the sterile deadlock in which a person insists that he or she did not make a choice?

A common approach is to point to ex-members who say that they now realize that they were brainwashed or under some kind of mind-control while they were in a particular movement; during the time that they were members, they assert, they believed that they were doing what they wanted, but now that they are no longer members, they realize that this was not really the case.

There are several problems with this as a 'proof' of brainwashing. First of all, it is quite possible that the ex-members are using concepts such as mind-control to explain what they now feel was a mistake. Second, research has shown quite clearly that it is those who have been deprogrammed who are most likely to say that they now realize that they were brainwashed, while those who leave voluntarily are very unlikely to make such a claim – and, it may be noted, part of the deprogramming process involves *telling* de-programmees that they have been brainwashed.

Third, however, I am not convinced that the persons themselves – either as believers or as ex-believers – can be the final arbiters when others who knew them before the event insist on an alternative account of their ability to judge what has been happening – although, of course, what converts and ex-converts say has to be taken into account. We cannot just accept the word of those who disagree with the members of the new religions without any further substantiation.

Furthermore, to a sociologist who sees people as part of a social context throughout their lives (we all are – need to be – born into an environment in which certain beliefs are assumed and transmitted to us from the cradle), it seemed obvious that no actions could be said to be reduced to *either* the result of a free, autonomous will *or* brainwashing; almost all situations are the result of more or less influence (positive acceptance or negative reaction) by others, be they parents, teachers, priests, peers, the media or smiling new friends offering a new Truth.

In trying to arrive at some solution to such difficulties, I came to the conclusion that, although we would certainly have to listen to what everyone was saying, and to observe the processes of recruitment in action (pontification from an armchair certainly could not be relied upon to produce any reliable resolution), it was necessary to approach the problem by looking not just at each individual case on its own, but also at a number of cases, taken together.

But, first of all, it was necessary to decide what might be meaningfully implied by such concepts as brainwashing, coercion, mind-control and free will – all of which are used in a variety of ways, and most of which are, philosophically, extremely slippery and, methodologically, not readily amenable to empirical investigation. I did not want to *start* from an assumption that people were either active or passive participants in conversion (as much of the literature did). I decided to start from the concept of choice. Bearing in mind the need to 'operationalize' the concept (that is, to devise a practical way of being able to recognize and test for the presence, or absence, of an abstract concept), it seemed helpful to think of choice as involving three interrelated ingredients:

- reflection (in the present);
- memory (of the past);
- imagination (of possible futures).

This led to the formulation: *A person can be considered to be making an active choice between two or more possible options when he or she can anticipate their potential existence and, in reflecting on these, is drawing upon his or her previous experience and previously formed values and interests to guide his or her judgement.* It is, of course, still possible for people to have been strongly influenced (by, say, their parents) in the values that they hold at a particular time; but my suggestion was that, in so far as people can *actively use or draw upon* their accumulated 'input' (and genetic dispositions) *at a particular time*, we can talk meaningfully of their making a choice. Conversely, if other people somehow manage to prevent their considering an otherwise available future alternative (such as continuing at university), then we might say that the person's capacity to choose had been reduced – or even removed.

Following from this definition, it is possible to isolate four variables that would have to be considered if we were to attempt to assess the extent to which a person is making a choice. First, there is the *person* (the potential recruit) with his or her predispositions; second and third, there are *alternative futures* (joining the new religious movement or continuing, as before, in the 'outside' society); and fourth, there is the *social context* within which the decision is reached – in this case, a Unification workshop.

If a movement were to lie about its beliefs and practices, then a decision based on inaccurate knowledge about one of the alternatives might not be the same as one based on more accurate knowledge. This in itself would constitute *deception* rather than mind-control. We might talk of brainwashing, mind-control, or undue influence occurring according to the extent to which the fourth variable, the social context, is instrumental in determining the outcome. If, *whatever* the previous beliefs, dispositions or expectations about their future happened to be, people inevitably became Unificationists once they were successfully lured into a Unification workshop (as has, indeed, been frequently claimed to be the case), then we might seriously consider that it was not they who were making the choice (unless we were to believe that the alternative that the movement was offering was irresistibly attractive – which most of us do not).

In fact, I found (and other researchers have come up with similar findings[2]) that 90 per cent of those who got as far as attending a Unification workshop did *not* become Unificationists – that is, the workshop was at least 90 per cent ineffective. The worskshop guests were perfectly capable of deciding that the movement was not for them. The range of both positive and negative reactions to the movement, its teachings and its members, clearly indicated that each guest was capable of reacting in his or her own special way to the alternative that was on offer – and by far the most common reaction was rejection, although only a minority expressed strong dislike or disapproval of the movement (in fact, several of the non-joiners claimed that they had developed a greater understanding of God and/or their own religion through their experience of the workshop).

In other words, the large number of people who seemed immune to the Unification offer, and the impressive variety of their reactions, suggested that the social context was not sufficient to account for the outcome of a stay at the Unification workshop. It seemed clear that it was, rather, something that the potential recruits 'brought with them' that was to be responsible for the decision whether or not they would become Moonies.

It might be proposed that there was a biological difference separating the joiners from the non-joiners, the former being the more susceptible to lack of sleep, variations in diet and such like. I could, however, find no evidence that people's *brains* were being affected to the extent that they would no longer be able to reflect on the possibilities open to them in the light of their past experiences, hopes, values and so on. A more difficult question concerned a differential susceptibility of their *minds* – whether the Moonies were somehow able to control the thoughts of some of their guests, even if they were unable to control the thoughts of those who rejected the movement.

There are several traps that people are likely to fall into when considering the practices of apparently strange groups. These are traps which, if we wish to be honest and fair, we must try to avoid in our assessment of the new religions, whatever our personal preferences may happen to be. I have already briefly mentioned the epistemological confusions that can arise out of assuming that we can, on the one hand, prove religious beliefs to be true or false, or, on the other hand, prove that observable behaviour is not amenable to systematic inquiry and that anyone's *opinion* on such matters is equally valid. Related to these confusions is the belief that some kinds of behaviour are necessarily more 'natural' and/or God-given than other types of behaviour. I am not suggesting that we cannot decide that we prefer one kind of behaviour or set of social customs to another set, but to insist that our own behaviour is more *natural* than other people's is usually to display (at least) an ignorance of anthropological and historical knowledge. We certainly know that people from other cultures have often considered the beliefs and actions of the conventional Christian missionary to be extremely unnatural.

The assurance that one's own behaviour is both natural and right can lead to the most blatant use of double standards in judging the behaviour of others. This is often revealed in the use of evaluative concepts that laud the behaviour of 'us' and denigrate exactly the same behaviour in 'them'. Examples used by both the new religions and their opponents are too numerous to list, but it is interesting to note the disparate ways in which the hands of God and Satan are seen to work from the points of view of the antagonists.

A final trap that I wish to mention is that of assuming that the differences between them and us are far greater than they may, in fact, be. Quite often 'bad' actions/beliefs are noted and assumed typical of members of 'it', and not noted and/or assumed atypical of 'us'. An obvious example would be that the suicide of a member of a cult would almost invariably be reported *as* the suicide of a member of a cult; the suicide of an Anglican is unlikely to be reported in headlines proclaiming that the victim was an Anglican.

The point I wish to make is that, if we want to learn about the characteristics of a particular group, unless we make direct comparisons between the new religions and the population as a whole (or more helpfully, those of a similar age and social background), we are not going to get information that we can *relate* to the group per se. If we read about cultists committing suicide more frequently than we read about Anglicans doing so, it is not altogether difficult to understand why we might grow to suspect that the new religions induce suicide in their members. If, however, we find a smaller percentage of cultists commit suicide than do non-cult members of the same age and social background, we may wonder whether there is something about the movements that *prevents* people committing suicide. Of course it may be that the movements attract those who are unlikely to commit suicide, but now the question is at least raised to be answered.

One reason for my making this point at such length is that it has frequently been asserted that the new religions are particularly successful in recruiting people who are, in some sort of way, particularly suggestible – perhaps because they are rather pathetic, inadequate or passive persons, or those who have had unhappy experiences and who are looking for a refuge from the difficulties of the world.

Findings of Research

When I began my research, I admit that I did suspect that this could, indeed, be the case. I compared four groups: the population as a whole, a 'control group' of young adults of the same age and from roughly the same background as the Moonies, a group of people who went to a Unification workshop, and the Moonies themselves. I hypothesized that I would find the control group most 'normal', the workshop group 'slightly peculiar', and the Moonies the most 'peculiar'. 'Peculiar' is not, of course, a very scientific term, but I was concerned to look at a number of variables such as unhappy childhood, divorced parents, a history of psychiatric disturbances (including perhaps, a suicide attempt), being unemployed, doing badly or erratically at school, or having no prospects for the future.

What I found was, however, that so far as most of these variables were concerned, it was a sub-group of the workshop attenders who did *not* join – or who joined for a very short time (a week or so) and then left – who turned out to exhibit the most 'pathetic/peculiar' characteristics. In other words, those who might seem particularly susceptible to suggestion might get as far as investigating the Unification Church, but they were very unlikely actually to commit themselves to full-time membership for anything but a few days – when they would be perfectly capable of deciding that they did not want to continue their association with the movement.

Who, then, were the people who joined? Their average age was 23; men outnumbered women by 3:2; they were disproportionately from the middle-middle and upper-middle classes; from 'good' families in which the values of duty and service to others were more likely to be found than those of earning money; they tended to be of above average intelligence and to have done well, although not brilliantly, at school; many had started, completed, or were planning to attend university or some kind of further education. They were more likely than either the control group or the non-joiners to have been brought up in homes in which religion was important, and to have believed in God at the time of their visit to the workshop. And they tended to be extremely idealistic. But they were doers, not drifters. They wanted to *do* something to make the world a better place, but had been unable to find a way of playing such a role in the wider society. Among the characteristics that seemed to offer the greatest 'protection' were atheism and (to a lesser extent) a strong commitment to another belief, and/or a happy and stable relationship with a partner.

I do not want to suggest that the workshop did not play an important part in persuading recruits to join the Unification Church; few (but nevertheless a few) have joined without attending one. At the workshop the Unificationists offered potential converts a loving community of like-minded 'brothers and sisters'; they made utopian promises about the restoration of the kingdom of heaven on earth and the role that the guest could play in this procedure. I am not even suggesting that converts deliberated rationally about what they were doing – they were quite likely to be swept along by the enthusiasms of the occasion – but *only* when there was some kind of 'fit' between the sort of things that they were *already* predisposed to be looking for or to feel at home with. They may not all have made a choice in a hard, calculating sense, but, I believe, they had made a choice in a softer sense; they felt 'at home' – that at last they had found the answers that they had been looking for, and that the conventional churches had seemed to be unable to give them. And, let it be remembered, if the alternative that the Unification Church was offering its guests did not seem to make sense to them in the light of their predispositions and previous experiences, they simply did not join.

There have always been those who, having discovered a new truth (or rediscovered an old truth), want to share their important knowledge with others. This, in itself, is not necessarily a 'bad thing'. So far as my personal experience goes, I have certainly felt myself under pressure from several of the groups whom I have studied. Unificationists have quite definitely tried to influence me and some dropped some rather ominous suggestions about what might happen to me if I did not take advantage of the opportunity which I had been lucky enough to have to learn about the movement. But evangelical Christians have chased my soul with just as much ardour and have warned me, with just as much foreboding, of Satanic repercussions if I did not give myself to Jesus – *their* Jesus.

Although both movements would vehemently deny any similarity, it is possible that the recruitment methods of another very visible new religion that has been (successfully) accused in the courts of brainwashing, the International Society for Krishna Consciousness (ISKCON), have been fairly similar to those of the Unification Church with respect to intensity.[3] It is also the case that, for some time now, both movements have been increasingly selective about whom they are prepared to accept as full-time members – partly because they have learned through bitter experience that unstable recruits can lead to their being blamed for the instability and any unfortunate occurrences that might subsequently happen as a result (they would say) of that prior instability. Both movements (especially ISKCON) have also become more insistent that potential members should wait some time before they commit themselves to a full-time membership. At the same time, both groups (and several of the other new religions) have recruited a growing number of members who, while sympathetic to the movements' beliefs and goals, do not dedicate their whole lives to the movements. These 'associate' members are more like members of a congregation, while the more fully committed members can be likened to priests, nuns or ministers.

A further aspect of the mission of several of the movements that should, perhaps, be mentioned is that they will frequently make contact with people, not in order to try to convert them, but in order to win their friendship or sympathy either for the movement or for one or more of its ideals. A popular method for this kind of mission has been the sponsorship of conferences on a variety of subjects, but very commonly, on the themes of peace and the synthesis of science and religion. Examples of movements that have organized such conferences within the past decades would be the Brahma Kumaris, the Church of Scientology, the Divine Light Emissaries, Sai Baba, the International Society for Krishna Consciousness, and perhaps most frequently, and conspicuously, the Unification Church, which built up networks of scholars, theologians, ministers, journalists, politicians and military personnel, who have shared and hoped to promote certain common interests – even if they do not agree with the movement's theology.

Of course, what applies in the case of the Unification Church and ISKCON does not necessarily apply in the case of other new religions, but the *method* of assessing their method is, I believe, a valid one – or, at least, more valid than that used by many so-called specialists who have, in my opinion, caused a lot of unnecessary anxiety and harm through their sweeping, and frequently inaccurate, descriptions of the new religions and their recruitment practices.

Some of those who read this paper may come to the conclusion that I have been irresponsible by playing down the potential problems that may be inherent in the practices of the new religions. Let me repeat that I do believe that it is possible for people to use unacceptable methods in order to further their own organization's beliefs and/or goals, and that these beliefs and goals (and the means used to attain them) ought to be scrutinized and, in some cases, controlled by the wider society. However, I also believe that those of us who wish to sit in judgement on the beliefs and practices of others should be as honest with ourselves, let alone with them, as is possible, given (and recognizing) both the limitations *and* the potentials of our knowledge.

It is understandable why the parents of those who join the new religions might be highly suspicious of the movements' motives and their methods, but if a democratic society wants to ensure that its young adults continue to lead a more conventional life, it might like to look at some of the reasons why a few of the movements do manage to persuade a few young people that they have something to offer that society has not, for little that is constructive will result from merely accusing the new religions of using unfair methods in their recruitment. The same advice might be given to the conventional churches.

This paper is an adaptation of one published in Allan R. Brockway and J. Pul Rajashekar (eds), New Religious Movements and the Churches *(Geneva: WCC Publications, 1987).*

Notes

1   Eileen Barker, *The Making of a Moonie: Choice or Brainwashing?* (Oxford: Blackwell, 1984).
2   See, for example, Marc Galanter, 'Psychological Induction into the Large Group: Findings from a Modern Religious Sect', *American Journal of Psychiatry*, Vol. 137 (12), 1980.
3   E. Burke Rochford Jr, *Hare Krishna in America* (New Brunswick, NJ: Rutgers University Press, 1985).

Chapter Five

TURNING WITHIN

Paul Heelas

The New Age movement represents several very different dynamics, but they thread together to communicate the same message: *there is an invisible and inner dimension to all life – cellular, human and cosmic. The most exciting work in the world is to explore this inner reality.* (Bloom 1991, p. xvi)

Setting the Scene

In Britain, as well as elsewhere in northern Europe, it appears that the number of those participating in institutionalized Christianity has been declining fairly rapidly. It also appears that the number of those who consider themselves to be either atheists or agnostics is not increasing so fast. If this is indeed true, it follows that the number of those who are (somehow) 'religious' in the territories beyond church and chapel is increasing in size. And in the territories beyond institutionalized Christianity, much supports the contention that a particular form of religiosity, namely New Age spirituality, is increasing in numerical significance.

The (apparent) growth of New Age teachings, practices and provisions, which claim to reveal a spiritual dimension integral to what it is to be human and (for many) to the natural order as a whole, sets the general context for this essay. More specifically, though, does this (apparent) growth involve, or depend upon, 'conversion'? To put the matter rather differently, could it be the case that involvement with what the New Age has to offer is better described – and therefore explained – in other ways?

Questions of this variety are prompted by a simple consideration: the term 'conversion' is rarely if ever used by those pursuing the inner spiritual quest. Having read countless books by New Agers (together with a number by sympathetic 'outsiders' intent on looking at what inner spiritualities have to offer), I have had to conclude that, for participants, the term 'conversion' is not at home here. This does not necessarily rule out the use of the term by academics studying

New Age spirituality. But the fact that participants do not use the term, instead favouring other ways of taking about their involvement, cannot simply be dismissed. Indeed, it might well have implications for the academic deployment of the idea of 'conversion'.

Before exploring the role (if any) of 'conversion' in involvement with New Age spirituality, it is necessary to provide some background information. The 'turn within' is first summarized. Attention is then paid to the vehicles – from new religious movements to books – which enable people to encounter inner spirituality. And then attention is paid to the question of whether New Age spirituality is a growth area. For if indeed this is the case, the question as to whether conversion has a role to play in growth becomes quite pressing.

New Age Spirituality

TURNING WITHIN

Three major themes run through the spirituality under consideration. The first is that the lives of the great majority of people are not working. This is because they are existing at the level of the 'ego' or 'lower self'. The ego is the result of socialization into the mainstream of society. It is what we are by virtue of being brought up as members of (conventional) families, schools or universities. It is what we are by virtue of being locked into all the demands, hopes and fears of business life and consumer culture. And the fact that people are locked into the 'externals' of life, it is claimed, means that they internalize all the defects of the 'systems' to which they belong. Family life only too readily transmits bad emotional habits; schools and universities generate anxiety and an over-reliance on the intellect; business life only too readily has a distorting and devaluing influence on personal life and familial relationships; consumer culture generates the pursuit of the superficial, the trivial. In short – the New Age literature is replete with criticisms of life in the conventional world – the ego level of functioning is regarded as serving to cultivate and then imprison people in a wide variety of bad habits. True, some New Agers are less critical of ego-operations and mainstream institutions than others. But without exception, the assumption is that something has to be done about what we are as products of modernity.

The second theme is that there is a very great deal more to life than is offered by mainstream institutions. The assumption is that we are all, at heart, spiritual beings. More generally, for many New Agers, the assumption is that spirituality is integral to the natural order as a whole, a dynamic of 'life' which runs through – and thus interfuses

– primal nature and humanity. And this spirituality is held to provide the very best that 'life' has to offer. To be in touch with inner spirituality is to experience tranquillity, peace, harmony, energy, vitality, power, 'aliveness'. It is to find wisdom or truth; to find one's 'purpose' in life. It is to be healed, 'centred'; to become 'aligned'. In short, those who are in contact with their inner spirituality are able to experience what it is to live as spiritual beings.

To experience life as laid down by mainstream institutions is one thing. To experience life as informed by inner spirituality is (apparently) quite another. And so to the third great theme of the New Age: that techniques are available to enable participants to turn within. The techniques themselves take a great variety of forms. There are all the different ways of meditating; there are techniques drawn from various 'pagan' spiritualities; there are those which have developed out of the psychotherapeutic and humanistic psychologies; one encounters body work; one even encounters things like fire-walking. But although the techniques appear to be very variegated, the majority are held to work in much the same kind of way. That is to say, they are seen to facilitate the turn within by enabling participants to exorcise the hold of the ego or lower self, the assumption being that once this is done participants quite naturally experience that spirituality which belongs to their very nature. Although, as we will see later, it is rarely if ever held that it is possible to eradicate the ego-level of functioning, especially on any kind of long-term basis, it is nevertheless widely maintained that it is possible to gain some degree of liberation from life infected by ego-operations. Thus some New Agers emphasize the importance of becoming aware of the bad habits of the ego, the act of awareness being taken to be liberating and enlightening. Or there is the strategy, found in many forms of meditation, of 'stilling' the chatter of the mind, spiritual awareness emerging as the chatter dies down. Then again, there is the strategy, especially associated with the more 'psychological' of practices, of 'working through' distressful ego-attachments and habits, this lifting the hold of the lower self and leaving 'room' for spirituality to come into evidence. Whatever the strategy – and there are many more, including working on the body to put the ego into its place by opening up dimensions over which it has no control – the basic idea is straightforward. It is possible to obtain enough 'distance' from the attachments and bad habits of the lower self to enter that spirituality which belongs to our very nature.

ENCOUNTERING THE TURN WITHIN

Background information is now provided on the topic of where people encounter the 'turn within'. Far from being centrally administered, the New Age 'movement' is composed of diverse modes of operation. Among other things, and without attempting to be too systematic, one can think of new religious movements (such as Scientology), communities (Auroville in south eastern India), ashrams (Osho's in Pune), covens (for those involved in New Age witchcraft or wicca), camps (as populated by shamanistic tribes in Wales), seminars (including those put on for business people), centres (the Open Centre or Dartington Hall), schools (Steiner), businesses (the Bank of Credit and Commerce International), gatherings (perhaps held at stone circles) and festivals (the Festival for Body, Mind and Spirit), clubs (Megatripolis), lectures (leading New Agers going on lecture tours), shops (as in Neal's Yard, Covent Garden), books, magazines, notice boards (advertising events), music and films. And, as we shall see in a moment, there are also the numerous 'new spiritual outlets'.

To cut things down to size, and to pave the way for our discussion of 'conversion', three key ways of encountering the turn within can be identified. The first concerns new religious movements. These are organizations which teach a particular version of what lies within, which advocate the use of particular ways of going within, which are exclusivistic in that they are critical of other ways within, which hope that people will become committed to what they have to offer, and which thus aim to expand their core membership. Being well organized, with headquarters, branches, full-time members to be employed and so on, new religious movements also have leaders, leaders who exercise (varying degrees of) authority to run their operations.

The second way of encountering inner spirituality concerns what shall here be called 'new spiritual outlets' (NSOs). Such outlets are typically run by an individual (or perhaps a small group of associates). Run from home (or perhaps a rented space), spiritual outlets are also characterized by the face-to-face encounter, the facilitator generally working with one client at a time. In addition, the client – more exactly the client's inner spirituality – is (apparently) accorded very considerable authority. To illustrate, briefly consider the following advertisement taken from *Common Ground*, the journal advertising 'Resources for Personal Transformation' in the San Francisco area:

Access Your Own Inner Answers, Guidance and Wisdom
Maryanna Blair

In our first session I will guide you and enable you to receive the rich, Knowledgeable answers that *Only Your Subconscious Mind* and your *Spirit* can give you! This access to your own wisdom comes to you through a process I've developed during 8 years of working with clients, and through *Your All Powerful* and *All Knowing Spirit* within you.

> These answers do not filter through my psychic mind's beliefs and understandings or values. Guidance is not influenced by anyone's interpretation or their ability to communicate it directly. *Your* answers, guidance and spiritual wisdom come direct to you, *Unchanged*, in the *Exact Language, Color* or *Image* that *Your Inner Spirit Knows* will produce the most complete *Multidimensional Impact On Your Clarity, Healing, Direction And Growth*

The advertisement, it can be added, ends with a private phone number.

Although those running new spiritual outlets might sometimes have learnt from (or even be affiliated with) new religious movements, NSOs are *not* NRMs. The person paying to have a series of one-to-one encounters with a facilitator is not joining an oganized religion, in particular as that person is quite likely to be drawing on other new spiritual outlets (either at much the same time or more serially). Furthermore, available evidence suggests that those running NSOs rarely attempt to establish a membership; and even more rarely – if ever – seek to have full-time followers. It would appear that those running NSOs (as with the illustration above) typically attach great importance to the autonomy of the spirituality of their clients. They are thus averse to exercising their own authority (in the fashion of leaders of NRMs) to claim that their practice is the best or only way within. Indeed, much suggests that they fully accept that many of their clients will also exercise their authority to draw on other spiritual outlets to pursue various aspects of their inner quests.

The third way of encountering inner spirituality to be discussed here concerns 'commodified' or 'mediated' spirituality. We are now in the territory of spiritual commodities: books, films, magazines, videos, CDs, artefacts (such as paintings or images), the implementalia of New Age healing, all purchased from designated spiritual shops or from more diversified stores. In contrast with new spiritual outlets, where the emphasis is very much on the face-to-face encounter, spirituality is now encountered in a form which can be taken home – typically to the armchair, where one can read the New Age book, watch the New Age video or listen to the music. Spirituality is commodified or mediated, then, in that it is 'carried' by way of concrete objects and the media.

GROWTH

Given the aim of this essay – to explore what, if anything, conversion has to do with the growth of involvement with New Age spirituality – we now turn to the matter of establishing that growth really is in evidence.

David Spangler (1993) writes that 'I have never met anyone engaged in any kind of New Age activity who has thought of herself or himself as having joined a new religion' (p. 79). This might be a somewhat exaggerated claim, but it serves to alert us to the fact that new religious movements and the quest for inner spirituality make pretty unhappy bedfellows. The basic reason is simple: those intent on the inner quest typically hold values and assumptions which are far from being catered for by new religious movements. The values of freedom, autonomy and creativity, for example, together with the assumption that authority lies with one's own experience, clash with the kinds of authority structures and codes of conduct perceived to belong to new religious movements. For this and other reasons, it is safe to say, new religious movements promising to facilitate the journey within are unlikely to prosper. True, organizations like Scientology continue to do relatively well (in the case of Scientology, not least in Hollywood circles), but we have to look elsewhere for evidence that growth is indeed the order of the day.

What, then, of new spiritual outlets? There is absolutely no doubting the fact that this is a significant area of development. An excellent index of growth is provided by the numbers of advertisements appearing in magazines like *Common Ground*. Thinking of *Common Ground* itself, the Winter 1979 issue contains some 300 entries. Twenty years or so later, the issue for Winter 1997/8 contains some 1,220 in the 'index' of advertisers. (It can be noted in passing that very few of the adverts in either issue are for organizations which can usefully be called new religious movements.) Or consider preliminary findings from research currently under way in the market town of Kendal in north-west England, there being at least 40 people making some or all of their livelihood out of running spiritual outlets. (Although longitudinal data is not available for Kendal, it is reasonably safe to say that prior to the 1960s, perhaps even later, there were no such outlets in the town.) Then one can consider my own monitoring (over the years) of events advertised on notice boards: just to give one representative example, the notice board in the Co-op in Settle, a small township in the Yorkshire Dales, now carries three adverts (including one for a healing festival), whereas up to a couple of years ago the board carried no such flyers. Finally, and thinking now of the most popular service provided by spiritual outlets, namely spiritual healing, Ursula Sharma (1995) reports European studies investigating the numbers who have 'ever used' complementary medicine, the figures being around 70 per cent for Belgium, 50 per cent for Finland, 30 per cent for Denmark and 28 per cent for Great Britain (pp. 16–17); another study reported by Sharma shows that the number of practitioners in this field in Britain grew six times faster than the number of GPs during the period 1978–81 (p. 13); and thinking of the United States, Michael Brown (1997) writes of 'the explosive growth in alternative health care ... now an industry that accounts for annual spending of $10–$14 billion' (p. 7). (Although it has to be accepted that much of what counts as complementary medicine has little to do with inner spirituality, evidence from a variety of sources suggests that those forms of complementary healing which are clearly spiritual have been increasing with the field as a whole, perhaps even faster.)

Then there are commodified and mediated forms of provision. And again, at least in Britain and almost certainly elsewhere, the picture is one of growth. Thinking first of my own monitoring, specialized New Age shops are increasing in number, few towns of any size not having at least one. Thinking second of publishing, recourse can be had to figures provided by Sara Selwood and Adam Thomas (1998, p. 9). Looking at percentage change in sales between 1993 and 1997, the greatest increase was in the geography and atlases category (185 per cent). This is followed by art (117 per cent), law and public administration (91 per cent), poetry (89 per cent), religion (83 per cent) and then the new age and occult category (75.5 per cent): not at the top of the list, but by no means an insignificant increase.

It is impossible, here, to go any more deeply into evidence of growth. Suffice it to say that all available indicators (and reasonably well-informed impressions) show that the number of spiritual outlets, spiritual shops, and commodified spirituality is expanding – a fact which contrasts with how those new religious movements which promise to cater for the turn within are doing. But what, if anything, has growth to do with conversion?

'Conversion' at Home

In order to establish what we are talking about, the argument has to begin with a brief discussion of the meaning of the term 'conversion'. The *OED* is as good a place to begin as any. Under the subheading 'Change in character, nature, form, or function' the entry runs,

The bringing of anyone over to a specified religious faith, profession, or party, esp. to one regarded as true, from what is regarded as falsehood or error. (Without qualification, usually = conversion to Christianity.)

And a slightly later entry reads, 'The action of turning, or process of being turned, *into* or *to* something else'. We can also consider A. J. Krailsheimer's (1980) observation that

Implicit in the idea of conversion is that of forsaking the past unconditionally and accepting in its place a future of which the one certain fact is that it will never allow the previous pattern of life to be the same again. (p. 5)

And I would also like to bring to consideration what Lewis Rambo (1987) has to say in his article in Eliade's *The Encyclopedia of Religion*. Having made the point that conversion is 'primarily a Jewish and Christian term', Rambo writes that 'conversion indicates a *radical call* to reject evil and to embrace a relationship with God through faith' (p. 73; my emphasis).

Taking my cue from Rambo, I want to develop the idea that 'conversion' is primarily at home in clear-cut theistic traditions like Christianity and Judaism. Taking my cue from the *OED*, the reason is that such traditions provide a clear set of beliefs and doctrines which enable people to turn, or strive to turn, '*into* or *to* something else'. 'Conversion', that is to say, is primarily associated with traditions which specify what one has to *believe* and what one must *become*; which highlight the difference between how one ought to live and other ways of life. Converts, with their new faith, might well struggle with their beliefs, but they are committed to attempting to change their lives. Converts, in other words, are converts precisely because they have adopted a tradition which *spells out* what *has* to be changed.

Undermining Conversion: The New Age as Spiritual Exploration

How does this 'classical' understanding of conversion – basically involving the demand for specified and radical change – fare if it is applied to characterize the New Age turn within? That is to say, how does it fare 'abroad', in the context of inner spirituality rather than theistic traditionality? The matter is now explored by reference to those described by Wade Clark Roof (1993) as 'highly active spiritual seekers' (p. 80). Attention is then paid to the possibility that many draw on New Age provisions for predominantly secular ends.

As portrayed by Wade Clark Roof and others, these are people who devote a considerable amount of time and energy to the task of experiencing spirituality. A key factor which serves to undermine the relevance of the (classical) use of the term 'conversion' is that few if any appear to think that it is ever possible to turn '*into* or *to* something else'. And an important reason why radical change is not on the cards is that it is widely maintained that the ego, the lower self, is highly skilled at ensuring its own survival. It wants to pursue its attachments, its pleasures. In the words of Enneagram worker Hameed Ali, 'the ego or personality is so incredibly entrenched' (as reported by Schwartz 1996, p. 406). The personality, as Ali also puts it, 'will do anything in its power to preserve its identity and uphold its domain' (p. 412). Spiritual disciplines might release the hold of the ego, but it reasserts itself time and time again: which is why Ali says that 'Ego death is a repeated and in time a continual experience' (p. 412). In short, the ego never goes for good – which means, of course, that a highly influential component of what it is to be human is never radically changed or converted. And, it can be added, the survival skills of the ego also explain why it is extremely rare to find New Agers who claim that they have changed and become fully and permanently enlightened.

The second consideration also has to do with the fact that few if any spiritual seekers appear to think that it is ever possible to turn '*into* or *to* something else'. But now attention is paid to the fact that inner spirituality is (apparently rarely) thought of as some *sui generis* 'end point' or 'something else' *to* which one can simply convert. Ali believes in 'essence', namely 'a more authentic experience of the true self' (as reported by Schwartz 1996, p. 375). And as Ali also says, 'There is no end to the development and unfolding of essence' (p. 412); again, 'Qualities of essence can be realized ... by steps and degrees' (p. 415). Or one can think of Shirley MacLaine and her observation that 'My quest in life is the most important thing. All of it is a quest and a question and none of it is answers. Every time I think I've got the answers I think it's different a week later' (cited by Sutcliffe 1997, p. 109). Then there is Gill Edwards, writing in her *Stepping into the Magic* (1993) that 'The whole point is our journey, not our destination' (p. 63). To give a final illustration, now from an academic, Wouter Hanegraaff (forthcoming) writes that the turn within is all about '*unlimited* spiritual evolution in which the Self *learns* from its experiences in many self-created realities' (p. 15; my emphases).

Rather than serving as a clearly demarcated realm to which one can convert, much New Age discourse suggests that spirituality is experienced as a realm which is unending; which never ceases to unfold. The language is of *exploration*. It is of obtaining an 'insight', then 'moving' to or 'encountering' a more profound level of 'awareness'. It is of 'growth', 'self-realization', 'seeking answers' by 'getting in touch with' ever 'deeper' aspects of spirituality, 'listening', 'discovery', the 'search', 'adventure' and 'journey': 'Life is a journey in which you learn from your experiences and grow as a person' as it is put by Wade Clark Roof (1993, p. 21); life concerns 'self-expansion', as Michael Brown (1997, p. 18) puts it, referring (for example) to a New Ager's conviction that 'the self is an infinitely expansive force' (p. 75); or one can think of the theme of M. Scott Peck's title, *The Road Less Travelled* (1990). Which raises the question: is this perpetual exploration and travelling really best described as conversion? Even that progressive conversion of the kind indicated by James Richardson's (1977) concept of 'conversion career'?

If the category of 'spiritual seekers' is worth its salt, seekers never finally convert – for then they would no longer be seekers. (And meditators could stop meditating!) To buttress the argument that they are engaged in unfolding exploration rather than conversion to some clear-cut 'something else', it can now be added that that 'something else' – that 'end point' or 'goal to be achieved' so crucial in constituting the act of conversion in the 'classical' understanding of the term – is not spelt out in terms of beliefs or pre-ordained codes of conduct. Generally speaking, although with varying degrees of emphasis, this is because New Age spiritualities are quite radically detraditionalized. What matters is trusting the authority of one's own experience rather than relying on the authority of transmitted tradition. Indeed, many New Agers are 'beyond belief', first-hand experience being taken to be greatly superior to anything which one might happen to believe in. In sum, given that New Age spiritualities are (largely) detraditionalized or post-belief, those involved cannot be thought of as converting to a particular set of beliefs or doctrines in the fashion of converts to traditionalized religion.

The 'classical' sense of conversion, I have been suggesting, does not really suit the territory of spiritual exploration and unfolding spirituality. The great majority of explorers do not believe that it is possible to effect radical change by effacing the hold of the ego. And the quest within, it seems, is typically seen as having no determinate point of accomplishment; no *sui generis* spirituality to mark 'conversion' to something radically different from where one has already got to. But even supposing that arguments of this variety do not convince, there is also the argument that the term 'conver-

sion' simply does not apply to much of what is going on as people encounter New Age provisions.

Invalidating 'Conversion': The New Age Serving This-Worldly Ends

To state the obvious, one can only consider applying the term 'conversion' to the turn within if indeed such a turn is in evidence. And
this prompts the question which is now attended to: could it be the
case that people draw on the New Age for predominantly (if not entirely) secular, this-worldly ends, rather than to pursue the spiritual
quest?

The first possibility is that New Age provisions are – on occasion –
treated consumeristically, as ways of pleasuring the self. This is the
view (among others) of Zygmunt Bauman. As he puts it in an especially arresting passage,

> The 'whole experience' of revelation, ecstasy, breaking the
> boundaries of the self and total transcendence – once the privilege
> of the selected 'aristocracy of culture' (saints, hermits, mystics,
> ascetic monks, *tsadiks* or *dervishes*) and coming as an unsolicited
> miracle, or as an act of grace rewarding the life of self-immolation
> and denial – has been put by postmodern culture within every in-
> dividual's reach, recast as a realistic target and plausible
> prospect of each individual's self-training, and relocated as the
> product of a life devoted to the art of consumer self-indulgence.
> (1998, p. 70)

On this account, New Age provisions merely serve to cater for what
'the experience-seeking and sensation-gathering life of the consumer . . . demands' (p. 72). New Age events serve as spiritual Disney-
lands, rituals evoking exhilaration, powerful memories, feelings of
community, experiences of fear or joy, perhaps even the sense of
being overwhelmed by the intensity of what is going on, or being
the centre of attention. Spirituality – if it is experienced at all –
merely serves to provide the icing on the cake, adding a sense of significance to the thrills and spills on offer.

It is impossible to say – given lack of research – whether consumer-
ized usage is widespread among those attracted to the New Age. It is,
however, highly likely that many of those encountering the New Age
through commodified and mediated spirituality are much more like
consumers than spiritual explorers. People listen to New Age music
to feel relaxed; read New Age books to fantasize about what life
could be like; watch New Age films to experience harmony. Further-

more, it is also likely that new spiritual outlets can be used consumer-istically: body work to ensure that one's body feels good, for example; or healing sessions to feel really vibrant and alive.

Consuming New Age provisions hardly adds up to spiritual con-version. And – somewhat more arguably – neither does drawing on the New Age to become more prosperous. There are now a large number of courses, seminars, trainings, books and programmes which claim to enable people to unlock their potential to become more effective at work and in otherwise (or magically) obtaining material goods. One reason why spiritual conversion does not seem to be in evidence is that many prosperity teachings and practices are largely presented in terms of (somewhat magical) psychological principles and assumptions, spirituality only being hinted at. Another, related, reason is that the emphasis is very much on ob-taining what the 'outer' world has to offer. Rather than concentrat-ing on enabling people to develop into becoming more 'fully fledged' as spiritual beings, spirituality (when it is introduced) is simply treated in instrumentalized fashion, important only for what it can produce.

Mention must also be made of another way in which New Age provisions can be utilized, again in a fashion which does not add up to spiritual conversion. Wade Clark Roof (1993) writes of 'the focus on the psychological', continuing that given this focus 'much attention is ... given to dealing with guilt, shame, depression, anxiety, tension, stress, and the like' (p. 130). Building on this obser-vation, there is absolutely no doubting the fact that virtually all New Age provisions – from new religious movements to books – devote a very considerable amount of attention to the travails of the ego or lower self. Although, as we saw earlier, it is widely held that the ego cannot be eradicated, this is not to say that difficulties embedded in the ego cannot be worked upon. This raises the possibi-lity, indeed likelihood, that large numbers draw on the New Age for what it has to offer with regard to ethicality, therapy and healing. Rather than being especially (or at all) interested in spirituality, their concern is with improving the quality of their ethical, psycho-logical and bodily lives.

To illustrate, consider the following passage from the conclusion of Tony Schwartz's *What Really Matters: Searching for Wisdom in America* (1996). Although Schwartz has been deeply involved in a range of New Age (and cognate) activities, there is no mention of his having realized his spirituality (either in the passage or else-where in his reflections on how he has developed). But he has changed (although not radically, as the last sentence makes clear) his sense of what his life is about.

My life has a sense of meaning, purpose, and direction that it
never had before.

   The first and foremost challenge is to be more aware, of myself
and others, to make more of my unconscious conscious, to see
more of the truth. Seeking the truth is sometimes painful and difficult, but it invariably makes me feel more authentic and more
grounded. It's not truth in some absolute sense that I'm after.
Nor am I primarily seeking to uncover the truth about others,
much as I appreciate it when I sense that people are talking to
me honestly, from their hearts. What I'm most committed to is
searching for my own truth. Like most people, I still often avoid,
or deny, or rationalize, or act out of habit, or look to blame
others in an effort to avoid truths that I find unpleasant or threa-
tening. (Schwartz 1996, p. 422)

Schwartz's encounters with the New Age have clearly encouraged
him to pursue a psychological-cum-ethical quest. His discourse
more than hints at something 'more' lying within, namely that
which 'grounds' him. But this is as far as it goes.

Undermining 'Conversion': The New Age and Autobiographical Incorporation

Thus far we have looked at how 'conversion' fares in two contrasting
ways: the activities of the committed spiritual seeker, and the activities of those who draw on the New Age for (predominantly) this-
worldly reasons. It remains to look at what goes on in between
these two contrasting modes of involvement.

   People here are not highly active spiritual seekers. Instead, they
turn to spiritual provisions when occasion demands, incorporating
spirituality into their lives together with all the other things they
draw upon to resource themselves. People here, it can also be
pointed out, are not simply utilizing New Age provisions for this-
worldly ends, more or less ignoring spirituality in the process.
True, those who incorporate spirituality into their lives often do so
for reasons of utility. But the fact remains – and this is where they
differ from the mere utilizers – they explicitly have faith in what
spirituality has to offer. That is to say, they explicitly acknowledge
the existence of the inner realm. And so to the question: does this
kind of involvement involve conversion?

   According to Robert Wuthnow (1989), 'the religion practiced by
an increasing number of Americans may be entirely of their own
manufacture – a kind of eclectic synthesis of Christianity, popular
psychology, Reader's Digest folklore, and personal superstitions,

all wrapped up in the anecdotes of the individual's biography' (p. 164). Although hard facts are not available, many have claimed that what can be called 'individuated religion' – or, perhaps better, 'autobiographical religion' – is on the increase. And it is not just religion, for, as Robert Wuthnow's reference to 'popular psychology' serves to indicate, religious incorporations can coexist with other ways of making sense of life.

As for the New Age, the claim is that people resource particular aspects of their (changing) lives by way of spiritual provisions, re-sourcing other aspects of their (changing) lives by way of other pro-visions. An excellent illustration is provided by Princess Diana. Thus the experts she drew upon to deal with the vicissitudes of the quality of her life include (in alphabetical order) the 'adviser', 'as-trologer', 'business motivator guru', 'clairvoyant', 'confidant', 'counsellor', 'exercise trainer', 'fitness teacher', 'gym trainer', 'homoeopathic doctor', 'hypnotherapist', 'lifestyle manager', 'masseur', 'mystic', 'New Age therapist', 'osteopath', 'psychothera-pist', 'sleep therapist', 'soothsayer', 'spiritual adviser', 'tarot-card reader', 'therapist', and 'voice coach'. Some of the experts, such as psychotherapist Susie Orbach, focused on dealing with the past; others, such as astrologer Debbie Fank, concentrated on what was in store in the future; yet others, including osteopath Michael Skip-with and masseur Stephen Twigg, were on hand to deal with im-mediate practicalities such as feeling right for an important event; and New Agers such as Anthony Robbins and Deepak Chopra were available primarily, it appears, to help her find an authorita-tive, spiritually informed, identity of her own.

Diana, I think it is fair to say, did not convert to the New Age. She certainly did not become a dedicated spiritual seeker. At the very best, she can be described as having 'partially converted' – this in the sense that although she came to find inner spirituality helpful for aspects of her life, she very much continued to draw on other re-sources (therapeutic, etc.) for other issues. But I am not especially happy with the term 'partial *conversion*', applied either to Diana or to all those others who draw on inner spirituality in this kind of way. My hunch – and hunch it has to be in the absence of adequate research – is that the incorporation of New Age provisions typically takes the form of 'this works for me'. Spiritual teachings and prac-tices become bound up with aspects of one's *own* autobiography; one's *own* needs, hopes and fears. And this is a very different kind of thing from conversion defined as attempting to change '*into* or *to* something else'. Indeed, one is inclined to suspect that incorpora-tion not infrequently involves the 'conversion' – the 'do it yourself' interpretation or experiential re-rendering – of spiritual provisions to suit the requirements, expectations and values of the person – an adjustment facilitated by the fact that, as have seen, new spiritual outlets (to which incorporators might well turn) generally attach great importance to the autonomy of the client.

Conversion and the Growth of New Age Provisions

Conversion has its home in contexts where people undergo quite radical change, acquiring faith (or a new sense of faith), new beliefs and values, and strive to live their lives accordingly. We have seen that there are a variety of reasons why this (classical) view of conversion – as specified and radical change – does not fare well in New Age circles. Most obviously, we have seen that many of those drawing on New Age provisions do not appear to take inner spirituality seriously, which means that the notion of spiritual conversion is simply not applicable. In addition, though, we have also seen that the term 'conversion', as classically defined, is ill-suited for describing the activities of spiritual exploration and incorporation.

This last point raises the consideration that the term 'conversion' should be broadened, to include – in particular – the turn within of the highly active spiritual seeker. Lewis Rambo (1987) is one of those in favour of broadening the term, to cover activities like the 'quest' (p. 75). But is this a useful thing to do? I think not. To use the term 'conversion' is to use a term whose cultural home (Judaeo-Christianity) is very different from that found in New Age circles. Unless the term is continually qualified, deployment in connection with the New Age can only too readily result in misleading impressions: in particular, that spiritual seekers think that it is possible to make some sort of leap of faith or belief, in the process undergoing some sort of radical change. Is it not much better for us to take our cues from how spiritual seekers themselves understand the turn within? And here, we have seen, the language is of exploration, realization, moving on; of only having faith in what experiences have to teach when the experiences themselves can always be enriched, deepened, transformed, even left behind; and of continually striving to exorcize the hold of the ego. On this account, explorers do not convert. They explore: and always with ego-operations standing in the way.

If indeed 'conversion' is ill-suited to characterizing much of what is going on in New Age circles, it follows that the kind of change described by the term has little (if anything) to do with the growth of New Age provisions. These provisions, the argument goes, are not proliferating because they are able to turn people into fully fledged members. The expansion of new spiritual outlets, as well as commodified and mediated provisions, it seems, has to be explained by

reference to other factors. We have to look at why spiritual explorers, those seeking to incorporate spirituality into their (diverse)
lives, and those utilizing New Age provisions for (predominantly)
this-worldly ends have grown in number. And that means that attention has to be focused on ascertaining what motivates people to
suppose that it is worth spending considerable time, energy and
money on seeking spirituality within, that it is worthwhile incorporating spirituality into their autobiographies, and that New Age provisions are worth utilizing for consumeristic, prosperity and
therapeutic purposes. And this leads us to psychological, sociological and cultural explanations of motivation: the thesis that the turn
within is a good solution to problems with identity (see, for
example, Berger *et al.*'s (1974) 'homeless mind' argument); the argument that the 'what works for me' mode of spiritual incorporation
is a fuelled by the pragmatic, 'it does not matter about belief'
outlook which is abroad in the culture; the role played by the
values and expectations of consumer, prosperity and therapeutic
cultures in encouraging people to utilize provisions for predominantly this-worldly matters (see, for example, Bauman's (1998)
consumer culture argument).

However, it is not so easy to ignore conversion (and therefore theories of conversion) *in toto*. One consideration, in this regard, is that
New Age provisions include new religious movements. And such
movements – with their full-time members, authority structures,
specific beliefs and practices – would appear, at least on occasion,
to be able to convert people as that term is classically defined. To
the extent that this is true, it is thus obviously possible to apply theories of conversion drawn from social psychology and other disciplines. Fortunately, though, since we are concentrating here on
growth, and new religious movements teaching the turn within are
not doing especially well, there is no reason, for present purposes,
to go any further into this complicated and controversial matter.

But there remains the consideration that significant numbers of
those who encounter New Age provisions other than those provided
by NRMs *come* to have faith in what spirituality has to offer. Spiritual explorers (excepting those who have been brought up as such)
have somehow to become *spiritual* explorers. And it is in this
regard, I think, that theories of conversion – better, *change* – can
have a role to play. But *only*, and this is the key point, if they attend
to what is going on. There is no point in applying theories (for
example of the intensive socialization or brainwashing varieties)
which purport to explain radical changes of belief and personality
when changes of this kind are not in evidence. But it is surely useful
to employ theories to attempt to explain what we know takes place:

specifically, that the practice of spiritual disciplines is often associated with participants coming to have what they consider to be
spiritually significant experiences. Theories, taken for example
from the psychological study of emotions, can thus have a role to
play in explaining the turn within. In sum, theories which are 'in
tune' with the reported nature of the spiritual quest surely deserve
serious consideration by those aiming to find out why New Age provisions can work – and thus grow.

The Turn to the Human as a Source of Significance

In conclusion I want to draw attention to another way of looking at
what is involved when people 'turn within'. The approach is provided
by an argument – running through the work of Georg Simmel, Arnold
Gehlen and (in many ways most systematically) in the Peter Berger of
The Homeless Mind (1974). Basically, the argument is that modernity
has been associated with significant numbers of people having to
turn to themselves as the key source of significance. For a variety of
reasons, which unfortunately cannot be gone into here, many have
become disillusioned with what the institutionalized order of things
has to offer, from traditional religion to political ideologies to the
nuclear family. The claim is that the institutional order no longer
succeeds in providing satisfactory ways of finding identity, purpose,
value in life. The feeling is that 'there must be something *more* to life';
that 'this cannot be all there *is*'. Accordingly, so the argument goes,
people have been thrown back on themselves. What matters
becomes a matter of what lies inside; one's psychology, one's personal
ethicality; the quality of one's emotions; the importance of being
authentic; the imperative of being honest about oneself; the value of
finding out *all* that one truly is and is capable of becoming.

What, then, are the implications of this argument for the spiritual
turn within? The claim is that those disillusioned with (much) of
what lies without are powerfully motivated to make the very best of
what their interior or personal life has to offer. And so it follows that
they could be attracted by what is offered by those (New Age) teachings and practices which promise to illuminate the very depth of
what lies within. New Age provisions – specifically NSOs together
with the commodified and mediated – it can then be claimed are
growing precisely because they allow those seeking their roots within
to experiment, explore the possibility that answers lie with spirituality, incorporate a spiritual dimension to the quest for personal
'growth', 'development' or 'realization'. 'I plan to continue my spiritual seeking; however, I am far from sure as to what it is that I am
seeking' says one of my students. Such people can probe – by way of

experience – to see what works, travelling further within if indeed effi-
cacious experiences unfold or insights emerge; and, for that matter,
retreating when their lower selves – intent on survival – intervene.

At the end of the day, the New Age turn within has a great deal to
do with the struggle for finding significance and 'wisdom' in life.
And who has ever said that one converts to wisdom?

References and Further Reading

The argument in this essay has had to cover a range of issues, not all
of which, unfortunately, have been attended to as much as they
deserve. For readers wanting more information on the New Age as
a whole, recent publications include (in alphabetical order of
authors), Michael Brown (1997), Wouter Hanegraaff (1996), John
Newport (1998), Chrissie Steyn (1994) and Michael York (1995);
see also the literature overview provided by Julia Iwersen (1999). I
have attempted to explore more specific issues attended to in this
essay in a number of publications. Presenting the publications to
correspond to the order of how the issues appear in the text,
Heelas (2000) looks at the question of what is happening beyond
church and chapel; Heelas (1996) provides information on the characteristics of the New Age, including its numerical significance;
Heelas (1999) looks at Diana's quest within; Heelas (1994) and
Heelas (1996) contain a survey of different theories of conversion
(it being noted that Heelas (1996) contains a discussion of involvement which differs in emphasis from what is argued here, attention
having previously been focused on explaining radical change when
indeed it takes place); and Heelas (1996, 2000) attends to the
human as a source of significance.

Bauman, Z. (1998), 'Postmodern Religion?' in Heelas, P. (ed.), *Religion,
Modernity and Postmodernity*, Oxford: Blackwell, pp. 55–78.

Berger, P. L., Berger, B. and Kellner, Hansfried (1974), *The Homeless Mind*,
Harmondsworth: Penguin Books.

Bloom, W. (1991), 'Conversion' in Bloom, W. (ed.), *The New Age: An Anthol-
ogy of Essential Writings*, London: Rider, pp. xv–xix.

Brown, M. F. (1997), *The Channeling Zone*, Cambridge, MA: Harvard University Press.

Edwards, G. (1993), *Stepping into the Magic*, London: Piatkus.

Hanegraaff, W. J. (1996), *New Age Religion and Western Culture*, Leiden: E. J.
Brill.

Hanegraaff, W. J. (forthcoming), 'New Age Spiritualities as Secular
Religion: A Historian's Perspective', *Social Compass*.

Heelas, P. (1994), 'The Limits of Consumption and the Post-modern "Religion" of the New Age' in Keat, R., Whiteley, N. and Abercrombie, N. (eds), *The Authority of the Consumer*, London: Routledge, pp. 102–15.

Heelas, P. (1996), *The New Age Movement*, Oxford: Blackwell.

Heelas, P. (1999d), 'Diana's Self and the Quest Within' in Richards, J., Wilson, S. and Woodhead, L. (eds), *Diana: The Making of a Media Saint*, London: I. B. Tauris.

Heelas, P. (2000), 'Expressive Spirituality and Humanistic Expressivism: Sources of Significance beyond Church and Chapel' in Sutcliffe, S. and Bowman, M. (eds), *Beyond the New Age: Exploring Alternative Spirituality*, Edinburgh: Edinburgh University Press.

Iwersen, J. (1999), 'Phenomenology, Sociology, and History of the New Age', *Nvmen*, XLVI (2), pp. 211–18.

Krailsheimer, A. J. (1980), *Conversion*, London: SCM Press.

Newport, J. P. (1998), *The New Age Movement and the Biblical Worldview*, Grand Rapids, MI: William B. Eerdmans.

Peck, M. Scott (1990), *The Road Less Travelled*, London: Arrow.

Rambo, L. (1987), 'Conversion' in Eliade, M. (ed.), *The Encyclopedia of Religion*, Vol. 3, New York: Macmillan, pp. 73–9.

Richardson, J. (ed.) (1977), *Conversion Careers*, London: Sage.

Roof, W. C. (1993), *A Generation of Seekers: The Spiritual Journeys of the Baby Boom Generation*, San Francisco: HarperSanFrancisco.

Schwartz, T. (1996), *What Really Matters: Searching for Wisdom in America*, New York: Bantam Books.

Selwood, S. and Thomas, A. (1998), 'Publishing and Bookselling in the UK', *Cultural Trends*, 29, pp. 1–36.

Sharma, U. (1995), *Complementary Medicine Today: Practitioners and Patients*, London: Routledge.

Spangler, D. (1993), 'The New Age: The Movement towards the Divine' in Ferguson, E. (ed.), *New Age Spirituality: An Assessment*, Louisville, KT: Westminster/John Knox Press.

Steyn, C. (1994), *Worldviews in Transition*, Pretoria: Unisa.

Sutcliffe, S. (1997), 'Seekers, Networks, and "New Age"', *Scottish Journal of Religious Studies*, Vol. 18 (2), pp. 97–114.

Sutcliffe, S. (1998), ' "New Age" in Britain: An Ethnographical and Historical Exploration', unpublished PhD, The Open University.

Wuthnow, R. (1989), *The Struggle for America's Soul: Evangelicals, Liberals and Secularism*, Grand Rapids, MI: William B. Eerdmans.

York, M. (1995), *The Emerging Network: A Sociology of the New Age and Neo-Pagan Movements*, Lanham, MD: Rowman and Littlefield.

Chapter Six

THE ROAD TO DAMASCUS: GLOBAL DIMENSIONS OF RELIGIOUS CONVERSION TODAY

Paul Freston

Globalization and Conversion

Religious conversion today needs to be discussed in a global perspective. All too often, however, this global perspective is absent, not only from discussions of conversion in general but even, ironically, from much literature on globalization. This is either because studies of globalization disregard religion altogether, or because they discuss it in the abstract, in apparent ignorance of what is happening on the ground. By 'on the ground', I mean basically in the Third World, which has two-thirds of the world's population.

One of the key questions for a discussion of conversion today, therefore, is what happens to conversion under globalization. Discussions about religion under globalization must take into account what has actually happened to Christianity in recent decades: recession in Europe and stagnation (masked by high-visibility political and media activity) in the US have been countered by the expansion of evangelicalism (at the expense largely of nominal Catholicism) in Latin America and impressive growth of all forms of Christianity in Africa and the Far East. But the only significant non-Western religious phenomenon that has impinged on Western academic consciousness is Islamic fundamentalism. Peter Beyer's 1994 book on religion and globalization, the major academic work so far, has five case studies: the New Christian Right in the US, liberation theology in Latin America, militant Islam in Iran, Zionism, and religious environmentalism. There is nothing on the growth of largely Pentecostal Christianity in the Third World which has transformed Protestant evangelicalism, along with Catholicism, into the first truly global religions. The constitution of a global Christianity is often ignored because it has occurred mostly independently of

77

Western initiatives. The same could be said for leading scholars of globalization such as Robertson (1992) and Waters (1995), even though both specifically discuss religion.

This omission, and the tendency to treat religion as an undifferentiated entity, may explain the strange feel of parts of Beyer's work. Are we heading towards a cultural 'religion of humanity' as the typical religion of the future, he asks. This Comtean-sounding question is surprising in view of what is happening on the ground in the Third World. The religion of the future, if at all unified, is more likely to be a recognizable evolution of an existing tradition, for which the main candidates are Catholicism, Islam and evangelicalism.

For many students of globalization, it seems as though a globalized world must either lead to religious relativism or to clashing fundamentalisms. A recent text by the Italian sociologist Enzo Pace (1997), published in a major work on religion and globalization in Brazil, is another example of the problem. He says globalization weakens the symbolic limits of belief systems, which leads to openness to cultural miscegenation. The rigid symbolic frontiers between religious fields disappear, as do the frontiers between religion and magic, and between religion and the new secular self-help beliefs. Globalization favours loss of memory of the traditions. Believers desert the religious institutions. Religion is freed from institutional control and returned to individual free enterprise.

I would say that for most of the Third World this is very unrealistic. Huge numbers still look to religion to provide a community. An over-emphasis on individualization and *bricolage* in religion seems too parochial when viewed from the Third World. What seems much more likely is that one or a few of the recognized religions will expand and become really global. Of course, they will undergo transformations during this process, but they will still be recognizably part of those traditions as we know them.

In addition, sometimes talk by globalization theorists about the effect of globalization on the 'religious traditions' gives the impression that the latter had never been subject to change before. An antidote to that, as far as Christianity is concerned, is Andrew Walls' work. He contrasts the serial expansion of Christianity with the progressive expansion of Islam (1995). Whereas the latter has spread out from a constant heartland, Christianity has been subject to periodic shifts in its demographic and geographical centre of gravity. This is because advances beyond its periphery have been countered by recessions in the old heartlands. As a result, Christianity is repeatedly coming into creative interaction with new cultures. In 1900, more than 80 per cent of professing Christians lived in

Europe or North America. Currently, more than 60 per cent live in Africa, Asia, Latin America or the Pacific (Walls 1992, p. 571).

In another work (1990), Walls talks of conversion in analogy with translation. Translation means something new is brought into a language, expanding it, but it also takes the material to realms it never touched in the source language. Similarly, conversion is not about substitution but about transformation, the turning of the old to new account. To what new account is evangelicalism being turned as it travels around the world?

Walls imagines a time-travelling researcher from Mars who visits Earth periodically to study Christianity. In each visit, he looks at a mainstream expression of the faith in that period: Palestine AD 37, Nicaea 325, Ireland 600, Great Britain 1840, Africa 1990. The descriptions Walls gives show the immense diversity of cultural expressions, theological emphases and ritual and social practices of each 'heartland' of the faith throughout history.

In Latin America, religious conversion is becoming more and more an accepted thing. It takes place in various directions among many different faiths, but by far the main beneficiary is evangelical Christianity, especially in its Pentecostal forms.

Why has evangelical Pentecostalism been successful as a global culture? I want to suggest an emphasis culled from diverse sociological, historical and missiological sources: evangelicalism has been a globalization from below.

Different strands point in this direction. If the Reformation concept of 'calling' led in the end to the 'Protestant ethic' which contributed to the 'iron cage' of bureaucratic rationality and the globalization of rationalized capitalism and the nation-state, the pietistic reconception of 'calling' led to mission and the globalization of voluntaristic Christianity. Mobilization for mission at the end of the eighteenth century was part of a profound shift in the social and discursive place of religion, one which presupposed a distinction between the public and private spheres. As for Pentecostalism, one of the high points of Harvey Cox's recent book (1996) is the contrast between the 1893 World's Parliament of Religions (an élitist white project of a refined Pentecost supported by the 'higher' religions) and Azusa Street (an exuberant black project linked into worldwide 'primal' religiosity). Unlike élite Western Christianity, which dialogues with the so-called 'world religions', popular religiosity in the West is much closer to the 'primal religions'. The growth of the Church in Africa, as Bediako (1995) says, has reminded us that primal religions have provided the background of faith for the majority of Christians throughout history.

Pentecostalism became globalized very quickly through the

international networks of counter-establishment religion. Key factors were the many American missionaries in contact with events at home, and the many immigrants in the United States in contact with their homelands and with countrymen elsewhere. Chile, Mexico and Brazil respectively are examples of these three routes.

We might say, therefore, in a Third World reading, that Pentecostal salvation came indeed from America, but from its underside. Born amongst the poor, blacks and women, it was exported at virtually no cost, often by non-Americans, bypassing the usual channels (religious and otherwise) of American wealth and power. It is precisely this counter-establishment Western Christianity that has become the most globalized.

Christianity has always had a global project (though often obscured), and its Pentecostal version was the most likely to spread once the Third World had indigenized the faith. A recent survey of evangelical institutions in Greater Rio de Janeiro discovered that, of the 52 largest denominations, 37 were of Brazilian origin, virtually all Pentecostal. While only 61 per cent of all evangelical churches were Pentecostal, 91 per cent of those founded in the previous three years were (Fernandes 1992). Greater indigenization accompanies greater pentecostalization. If post-modernity is essentially 'incredulity towards metanarratives' (Lyotard), then the globalization of Pentecostalism, perhaps the fastest growing metanarrative in the world, questions Eurocentric interpretations of our global future.

The future of religion lies not only in association with localist opposition to globalizing trends, but also as personal choice within the thrust of globalization itself. David Martin (1995) sees the salvageable essence of secularization theory as the process of social differentiation which breaks up monopolies, leading to a pluralism which vitalizes the religious field by competition. In this context – which characterizes ever larger parts of the globe – of individualism centred on expression of the self and putting together of fragments of traditions, evangelicalism seems well equipped to flourish, since it takes elements of expressive individualism but controls them with moral obligation and community loyalty.

To give some idea of what is happening in Latin America, we can use the already cited survey of Greater Rio de Janeiro carried out in 1992. Protestant churches totalled 3,477. Between 1990 and 1992, a new church was registered for every weekday. In one Catholic diocese there were over twice as many Protestant places of worship as Catholic, and in the poorest districts the ratio was seven to one. Protestantism is 'an option of the poor' (Fernandes), a reference to the less successful Catholic 'option *for* the poor'. The needier the district, the more Protestants: 20 per cent in the poorest areas versus 6 per cent in the rich South Zone. Protestantism is an 'option' because it results from conversion, and 'of the poor' because it grows more quickly (though not exclusively) among them and through 'institutional means which are equally "poor"' (Fernandes 1992, p. 14). Of new churches, 91 per cent are Pentecostal. Of the 52 largest denominations, 37 are of Brazilian origin (virtually all Pentecostal) and nearly all the rest have long been autonomous. 'It no longer makes sense to think of Protestantism as a "foreign religion"' (Fernandes, p. 19). Protestant religion is *national*, *popular* and *rapidly expanding*, 'perhaps the most important movement for changing mentalities in contemporary Brazilian society' (Fernandes, p. 25).

Protestantism is pre-eminently of the poor and, especially, the less educated. It is well represented among blacks and mestizos.

Explanations for Conversion to Pentecostalism in Latin America

Why does Pentecostalism grow in Latin America? The debate is often a weapon in political and religious polemic, helping to stigmatize it as illegitimate or pathological.

Catholic analyses are influenced by post-conciliar ecumenism. Since the 1980s, however, it is again acceptable to show concern over Protestant growth by talking of the 'sects'. A leading Catholic newspaper in Brazil talks of an 'evangelical offensive' whose 'impressive bellicosity' uses the 'ignorance' of the people.[1] Another journal, linked to the Brazilian Bishops' Conference, says the 'evangelical sects ... almost always lead ... to a conformism and conservatism ... which favour charlatanism'. The analyses reveal a static view of culture in which religions have people and not vice versa. 'Sects' such as the Assemblies of God (in fact a huge denomination with at least seven million members) are 'movements rather than churches' and seduce converts by all methods, affirms the president of the Bishops' Conference.[2]

Seeing itself as the (most) legitimate religious institution, much of the hierarchy sees the 'sects' as a failure in its own work. Selective imitation is proposed. However, 'much of the church had been [imitating selectively] for decades, [which] helps explain why many Catholics felt they needed a second reason, political in nature, to account for the multiplication of evangelicals' (Stoll 1990, p. 34). The conspiracy theory was resurrected: the 'sects' grow thanks to politically motivated American money. In Brazil, this theory had emerged with increasing Vatican power over the Church in the late nineteenth century. In the 1930s, the leading (conservative) archbishop viewed Protestant expansion as a plot by American millionaires. In the mid-1980s, the Bishops' Conference (no longer conservative) was suspicious of CIA involvement.[3] According to a 1991 Latin American report to the Vatican, 'the sects ... are promoted by interests foreign to our own life ... which gradually weakens the Catholic Church's power over the people ... The idea grows that there is no need to be Catholic ... to maintain the greatness of national identity.'[4] Even some progressives adopt a conspiracy theory, because their project depends on latently Catholic masses mobilizable in the base communities.

Explanations for the 'sects' portray the people as victims of propagandist methods or foreign money. Incapable of adapting a religion to their own needs, they should be protected by mother Church or the paternalist state. 'Sects' only grow because of pathologies, whether religious (Catholic pastoral deficiencies) or social (poverty, anomie). They are never seen as signs of health in the social body.

'Invasion of the sects' theory builds on facts. Protestantism has many foreign connections; the question is how important they are. Protestantism in certain countries (Central America) is more susceptible to foreign influence than in others (Brazil, Chile). But in personnel and money, Catholicism and historical Protestantism are more foreign.

Stoll (1990) for Spanish America and Fernandes (1981) for Brazil have made detailed analyses of the question. Fernandes concludes that, despite the tripling of missionaries after the 1964 military coup in Brazil, this has little to do with Protestant growths. Over a third of them work with Indians, 0.2 per cent of the population. Most faith missions are anti-Pentecostal. 'The churches which grow most owe little to international missions.'

Stoll focuses on the Christian Right in Central America. While recognizing the danger of missions being influenced by the religious Right, he says the importance of foreign personnel, money and TV programmes is exaggerated by protagonists and antagonists. The religious Right was resisted not only by principled opponents but also by established conservative missions who feared a backlash. 'Judging from where churches were growing rapidly, it seemed as if the recipe for success was for missionaries to leave' (Stoll 1990, p. 72).

Some interesting insights have come from anthropologists. They have treated Pentecostalism positively as compared with the situation of the poor, rather than negatively as compared with an intellectualist ideal of the social role of religion. 'Among those interviewed, the believers attracted my attention ... There was in them a restored dignity, despite the visible deterioration of their living conditions' (Novaes 1985, p. 7).

Recently, an English anthropologist has reflected on his research experience.

> What I experienced as Pentecostals' aggression was ... a challenge to the assumption of superiority ... [Pentecostals are shocking because] they are not submissive ... The white male from a rich country was put on the defensive by poor black women.[5]

This perspective is not general, however. A large part of academia still views Pentecostalism with dismay because it rejects the traditional Latin American model of the religious field and popularizes an alternative pluralist model. The latter is of mutually exclusive groups in competition, breaking with Brazil's historic model of *hierarchical syncretism* which combines non-exclusive affiliation with acceptance of Catholic institutional hegemony. Candomblé is called a body without a head, because the head is in Catholicism. But Pentecostalism is the first mass religion in Brazil consciously to reject the institutional force-field of the Catholic Church.

This multiplication of autonomous *sects* is seen by many authors as a search for solace in social crisis, and thus as a symptom of disease. But crises can also be seen as opening new opportunities (Levine 1991, p. 20f). 'Sects' would thus be a phenomenon of freedom, as in the historiography of the English Civil War. Rather than symptoms of disease, they would be signs of civil society freeing itself from ancient restrictions.

Another version of pathology theory links growth to political repression. There is a basis for this. Such rapid growth in Guatemala would have been unlikely without counter-insurgency. However, this does not explain why people turned to this particular option (the supply side), nor why most people in this situation did *not* convert (the micro level).

In Argentina, on the other hand, Pentecostal take-off occurred at redemocratization. Chilean and Nicaraguan Protestantism grew most rapidly during non-repressive left-wing governments. As for Brazil, Rolim asks:

> Is it pure concidence that an intensely sacral faith should arrive at a time [the 1910s] when the urban workers were being shaken by another experience [anarchism] producing workers' struggles? Was it exclusively religious motives which determined the Pentecostal leaders' arrival? (Rolim, 1985, p. 73)

Rolim dates Pentecostalism's take-off from 1935, 'when authoritarian measures began to stifle the workers' movements' (p. 80). It is a repeat of Thompson's theory for English Methodism (cycles of political activism, repression and retreat into religion), questioned by Hobsbawm, who suggested Methodism advanced concomitantly with radicalism. The evidence also does not support Rolim. The founder of the Christian Congregation went first to Buenos Aires and then to São Paulo, following the order of importance of the Italian diaspora. The Swedes of the Assemblies of God went first (following a prophecy) to Belém and spent years evangelizing the hinterland of the Amazon delta, arriving in São Paulo nearly twenty years later; hardly an intelligent plan to save Brazil from an imminent proletarian revolution. As to Pentecostal take-off, statistics point not to 1935 but to the late 1940s, a period of unprecedented democracy.

There is a better case for linking Pentecostal growth with economic crises. Although poverty is endemic, impoverishment is supposedly causing many to seek solutions in miracle-working churches. The 'health and wealth gospel' offers a 'religion of results'. The explanation is plausible. As in all cases of simultaneity, however, there are other possibilities: chronological coincidence; a third factor mediating the relationship; or economic crisis as a contributory but minor factor. A survey in Rio (ISER 1996) found only 4 per cent of new converts said financial problems were a cause of conversion.

For D'Epinay, the contrast between Argentina and Chile shows growth does not correspond to any socio-economic typology. Instead, influenced by dependency theory, he proposes a 'field of possibilities': the crisis of the 1930s made mass sectarian Protestantism possible. In Argentina, however, Peronism pre-empted it. Socio-economic destructuring is a necessary but not sufficient condition for growth (1975, pp. 93ff).

D'Epinay's key concept is anomie, normative and existential disorientation caused by social and spatial uprootedness. Traditional society is recreated in the *sect*. Should we conclude Pentecostalism is a life-jacket to be discarded later? The data suggest not. Tennekes found most Pentecostal migrants had arrived in Santiago long before (1985, p. 30). In Recife, Hoffnagel found many were Pentecostals before they migrated and many others spent years in the city before converting (1978, p. 40f). Since Brazil is now 70 per cent urban, anomie caused by migration could today be only a secondary factor. The rate of migration has diminished, while the rate of Pentecostal growth has increased.

Droogers (1991) talks of divergent and even opposing suggestions in the literature and concludes that an eclectic approach allows us to see these as paradoxes resulting from partial explanations rather than as intractable contradictions. Religion is ambivalent and offers different things to different people. This is wise: Pentecostalism is flexible and there is unlikely to be a single grand reason for its success. An eclecticism based on the ambivalence of religion must take into account not only political and economic but also social, cultural, ethnic and religious factors; not only the macro level (which social characteristics favour conversion) but also the micro level (why only some people with those characteristics convert); not only the appeal of Pentecostalism to men but also (especially) to women; not only the demand side (why people are ready to convert) but the supply side (what Pentecostals do to maximize their potential public). And it must ask not only why Pentecostalism grows so much, but why it does not grow more, and why some types grow more than others.

Social and cultural factors may be more important than political or economic ones. Social autonomy was important for Protestantism's capacity to prise open the traditional unity of Catholicism and cultural identity. Recent growth has reflected the expansion of pluralism and personal autonomy, making it respectable to change religion. Protestantism, says Martin, is successful because it is sociologically advanced and theologically 'backward': it separates faith from state power, corresponding to increasing social differentiation; but it also creates enclaves of the faithful where social experiments can be carried out (1990, p. 106).

Today, the demonstration-effect of Protestant growth in parts of the region on the weaker parts should not be discounted, strengthened by the sense of a cultural bloc; Catholicism was important in this unity, and its erosion also has regional repercussions.

But propensity to convert is not enough. As Bruce says, macrosociological analyses are incomplete because the population with the favourable characteristics is always much greater than the number who convert. To go further, we need the micro-sociology of personal relationships and social networks (1989, p. 247). Related to this is the 'supply' side: the favourable components of Pentecostalism itself. As *conversionist sects*, Pentecostal churches practise almost continuous proselytism, ideally involving every member. Equally important is the effect of competition, which stimulates constant innovation and localized supply (the poor have little mobility and a religious option available locally may corner the market).

A recent survey in Rio (ISER 1996) found 70 per cent of evangelicals were converts from another relgion. About one hundred thousand people are becoming evangelical every year in Greater Rio; of these, 61 per cent come from Catholicism, 16 per cent from Afro-Brazilian religions and 7 per cent from Kardecist spiritism.

The survey shows that half of the converts deny suffering from serious problems at the time of their conversion. Of those who say they did, sickness and family problems predominated, followed by alcohol. Financial problems were way down the list, even though most of the people concerned were poor.

Within the evangelical world, 25 per cent have already changed churches. These exchanges go in all directions, though Pentecostals are net gainers and historical Protestant churches net losers.

All this presupposes the capacity to communicate. Only religious people tend to see solutions to their economic problems in religious activities (Bruce 1990, p. 220). Pentecostalism is not only Christian but also close to Latin American popular religiosity, tuned in to an inspirited world.

This proximity is stressed by studies which try to account for Pentecostalism's success and the base communities' (CEBs) numerical weakness. Levine says the CEBs lack institutional flexibility, their discourse is alien, and they de-emphasize personal morality and healing (1991, p. 11f). Recent Catholic studies talk of conflict between progressive Catholic 'pastoral rationalism' and the 'popular symbolic universe' (Teixeira *et al.* 1993).

Mariz (1989) talks of similarities and differences. Both CEBs and Pentecostalism break with fatalism. Both develop dignity and the capacity to express oneself. Both represent religious rationalization and motivate to deal with poverty. In the long run, they will have similar consequences, despite their contrasting discourse. However, CEBs do not emerge spontaneously from the poor. They attract people who already have a sober lifestyle; Pentecostalism gives a sober lifestyle to those who do not have it. While Pentecostalism changes the values of popular religion, CEBs change its cognition. So Pentecostals do better because their cognitive assumptions are closer to popular culture, and leaders are from the same origin.

Burdick (1993) explores Pentecostalism's greater popularity in Brazil. First, CEBs attract the more stable and literate segments of the working class, while Pentecostalism accommodates the poor in general. CEBs reject a rupture with worldly identities, and participants' worldly status is on everyone's minds. Also, anonymity is harder in small groups. Liberationist discourse values literacy and articulateness, making the very poorest reluctant to attend. Pentecostalism, however, creates a liminal state in which normal social relations are suspended. Valuing the Spirit over the word enables illiterates to be leaders.

Second, married women have difficulty resolving domestic problems through the CEBs, not only because liberationism emphasizes macro-perspectives but because neighbourhood relations make them gossip-prone. In Pentecostalism, women find the supportive atmosphere of a group recruited on the basis of suffering.

Third, youths find progressive Catholicism requires a difficult balancing act regarding popular youth culture. With no transformative discourse, rivalries and status-rankings are transferred to the religious setting. But Pentecostalism permits a clear break with the culture of competitive sexuality and violence.

Finally, CEBs lack an effective counter-discourse to racism. Pentecostalism is 'darker' in membership and leadership. While not a racial democracy, it provides a better practical context for struggles for equality.

Accounts of growth must note what Pentecostalism offers its considerable female membership, looking beyond patriarchal rhetoric to perceive its 'revalorization of the material, psychological and spiritual currency of the family' (Garrard-Burnett 1993, p. 204). The advantages to poor women are financial, emotional and physical. Brusco (1993) says Pentecostalism helps women resocialize men away from the destructive patterns of *machismo*, even though (or precisely because) it maintains the rhetoric of male control. A new ideal of manhood is promoted, and an alteration in consumption patterns. Male aspirations are redefined to coincide with their wives'. The novelty is illustrated by Caldeira's work on the periphery of São Paulo. 'Women's projects are made much more for others [children, husband, home] ... Men's are invariably in the first person singular ... Their wives are never mentioned' (1984, p. 179ff). Pentecostalism's reconciliation of gender values (which middle-class feminism has not achieved) serves the interests of poor women.

Conversionist Mission from Periphery to Centre

One of the main religious changes of the late twentieth century has been the transformation of Pentecostalism into a global religion and the shift in its centre to regions distant from the historical heartlands of Protestantism. By 'centre', I mean not only numerical predominance but also the heart of its worldwide expansionist impulse. Conversion is now flowing once again, as it did during the primitive Church, from the periphery of world power to its centre, rather than vice versa.

It is true that current trends allow many religions to become globalized (as in the World Congresses of Yoruba Religion). But the scale of Pentecostalism is altogether different. Twelve per cent of

Ghanaians live abroad, and half of these have been through Pentecostal 'prayer camps' before emigrating (Van Dijk 1996).

Pentecostal expansion often follows diasporas (African churches
in Europe, Latin-American ones in the US). But apart from the Pentecostalism that accompanies emigration, there is also a Third
World missionary effort that goes way beyond the diasporas. Little
is known about the missionary movement of the new mass evangelicalism of the Third World, but by the end of the century it will
probably be larger than the First World missionary movement.

The main Brazilian church in this process is the Igreja Universal
do Reino de Deus (Universal Church of the Kingdom of God –
UCKG). Founded in a poor suburb of Rio de Janeiro in 1977, it is
now present in over 50 countries (Freston, forthcoming).

The social composition of the UCKG in Brazil is accentuatedly
lower class. While 45 per cent of the general population of Rio
earns less than two minimum salaries, the rate amongst UCKG
members is 63 per cent. Only 21 per cent of the population has less
than four years of schooling, versus 50 per cent of the UCKG.
Whites are 60 per cent of the population, but only 40 per cent in
the UCKG. This lower-class base is linked with enormous institutional power due to strongly hierarchical organization, political
strength (17 members in the Brazilian congress), financial wealth
(34th-largest private enterprise in the country) and media empire
(daily newspaper, over 30 radio stations and above all the third-
largest television network in Brazil).

While seeing itself as part of the Protestant community and heir to
the evangelical tradition, the UCKG also has links with traditional
Brazilian religiosity. In the words of one leader, 'We do not follow
a European or American evangelical tradition; we start from the religious practice of the people.' Or, in the opinion of the president of
the Brazilian Evangelical Association, the UCKG is a new syncretic
religion which mixes 'evangelical teachings, precepts of the medieval Catholic Church and Afro-Amerindian elements'.

Three cultural blocs account for well over 90 per cent of the
UCKG churches abroad:

- the Latin American bloc, which includes Hispanics in the US;
- the Portuguese-speaking countries;
- African countries and the African diaspora in Europe.

The Lusophone, Latin American and African worlds, with which
the Brazilian UCKG has cultural and/or linguistic links, provide
the vast majority of the worldwide membership. The non-Iberian
white world, Asia and the politically inaccessible Middle East
remain a challenge.

The UCKG began in England in June 1995, with a small church in the London Borough of Brixton. In October of that year, it bought the Rainbow Theatre in Finsbury Park for 4 million dollars, having previously attempted to purchase the Brixton Academy for 6.4 million dollars in the first half of the year. It now has some six churches in London and Birmingham. The attempt to buy the Brixton Academy shows the strategy with which the UCKG arrived in England. Brixton is the most famous black district of London. The small church functioning there is frequented almost exclusively by blacks. Even at the Rainbow, 90 per cent of the public is black. Although its pastors are mostly white Brazilians or Portuguese, the UCKG in England has made the black community its main target and thus comes close to the category of Afro-Caribbean church in the English religious world.

However, the UCKG shows awareness of the dangers of this strategy. It clearly wants the black community in Britain to be a beachhead into the country and not a prison. It is trying hard not to get entrapped in the 'Afro-Caribbean church' category. Thus, on the one hand the black community is cultivated as the initial target and, later, the mainstay of the membership. On the other hand, there is a growing use of Asians and whites in testimonies. It remains to be seen how easy it will be for the UCKG to achieve a more even racial balance in its membership. But it is clearly already playing an interesting role for the Afro-Caribbean community, whose churches are now affected by the drama of 'naturalization': the younger generation, born in the country, is impatient with the old traditions and in search of its own identity. Another factor is that almost half the young people of Caribbean origin marry non-blacks. In this context, the UCKG (with its exotic origin, message of success and self-respect, attempt to integrate the poor of all colours, and its predominantly white leadership) may be able to offer a halfway house between a traditional Afro-Caribbean and a white church.

In a recent book, an African theologian asks whether 'the modern Western world, in Christian recession but with increasing interest in the occult, [is so] impervious to the experiences of Christian transcendence recorded in the South?' (Bediako 1995, p. 166). Mass adoption of Christianity in Africa, he suggests, might have global relevance. Extending the argument, we might ask about a possible role for Brazilian Pentecostalism in any future re-Christianization of Europe. In ethnic, cultural and economic terms, Brazil is a bridge between Europe and Africa and its churches might have a bridging role for the Third World minorities at the heart of the developed West. Whether they can go beyond that and achieve a significant number of conversions amongst the native populations is still an open question. As a UCKG pastor in a First World country once wrote (Silva 1991): we shall

> have to wait and see how the [Universal Church] adapts to new cultures in which the people do not have the same fear of spirits ... but, following Jacques Ellul's ideas, they may find that new demons are lurking in the big cities of the world and in other cultures.[6]

Notes

1   *30 Dias*, October 1990, pp. 48–55.
2   Dom Lucas Moreira Neves, in the *Folha de São Paulo*, 9 February 1988.
3   *Veja*, 19 July 1990.
4   *L'Osservatore Romano*, 21 April 1991, p. 7.
5   David Lehmann, 'Problems of Method', mimeo, 1994.
6   The reference to the French sociologist Ellul, author of *The New Demons* (1973), is noteworthy.

References and Further Reading

Bediako, K. (1995), *Christianity in Africa*, Edinburgh: Edinburgh University Press.

Beyer, P. (1994), *Religion and Globalization*, London: Sage.

Bruce, S. (1989), *God Save Ulster! The Religion and Politics of Paisleyism*, Oxford: Oxford University Press.

Bruce, S. (1990), *A House Divided: Protestantism, Schism and Secularization*, London: Routledge.

Brusco, E. (1993), 'The Reformation of Machismo: Asceticism and Masculinity among Colombian Evangelicals' in Garrard-Burnett, V. and Stoll, D. (eds), *Rethinking Protestantism in Latin America*, Philadelphia: Temple University Press, pp. 143–58.

Burdick, J. (1993), *Looking for God in Brazil*, Berkeley, CA: University of California Press.

Caldeira, T. (1984), *A Política dos Outros*, São Paulo: Brasiliense.

Cox, H. (1996), *Fire from Heaven*, London: Cassell.

D'Epinay, C. L. (1975), *Religion, dynamique social et dépendance: les mouvements protestants en Argentine et au Chili*, Paris: Mouton.

Droogers, A. (1991), 'Visiones Paradójicas sobre una Religión Paradójica: Modelos explicativos del crecimiento del Pentecostalismo en Brasil y Chile' in Boudewijnse et al. (eds), *Algo Más que Ópio: una lectura antropológica del pentecostalismo latinoamericano y caribeño*, San José, Costa Rica: DEI, pp. 17–42.

Fernandes, R. C. (1981), 'As Missões Protestantes em Números', *Cadernos do ISER*, 10, pp. 27–84.

Fernandes, R. C. (1992), *Censo Institucional Evangélico CIN 1992: Primeiros Comentários*, Rio de Janeiro: ISER.

Freston, P. (Forthcoming), 'The Transnationalisation of Brazilian Pentecostalism: The Universal Church of the Kingdom of God' in Corten, A. and Marshall-Fratani, R. (eds), *Pentecostalism and Transnationalism*, London: Hurst and Co.

Garrard-Burnett, V. (1993), 'Conclusion: Is This Latin America's Reformation?' in Garrard-Burnett, V. and Stoll, D. (eds), *Rethinking Protestantism in Latin America*. Philadelphia: Temple University Press, pp. 199–210.

Hoffnagel, J. (1978), 'The Believers: Pentecostalism in a Brazilian City', PhD thesis, Indiana University.

ISER (Instituto de Estudos da Religião) (1996), *Novo Nascimento: Os Evangélicos em Casa, na Igreja e na Política*, Rio de Janeiro: ISER.

Levine, D. (1991), 'Protestants and Catholics in Latin America: A Family Portrait', mimeo.

Mariz, C. (1989), 'Religion and Coping with Poverty in Brazil', PhD thesis, Boston University.

Martin, D. (1990), *Tongues of Fire: The Explosion of Protestantism in Latin America*, Oxford: Blackwell.

Martin, D. (1995), 'Sociology, Religion and Secularization: An Orientation', *Religion*, 25, pp. 295–303.

Novaes, R. R. (1985), *Os Escolhidos de Deus*, Rio de Janeiro: Marco Zero.

Pace, E. (1997), 'Religião e Globalização' in Oro, A. P. and Steil, C. A. (eds), *Globalização e Religião*, Petrópolis: Vozes, pp. 25–42.

Robertson, R. (1992), *Globalization*, London: Sage.

Rolim, F. C. (1985), *Pentecostais no Brasil*, Petrópolis: Vozes.

Silva, M. (1991), 'A Brazilian Church comes to New York', *Pneuma*, 13 (2), pp. 161–5.

Stoll, D. (1990), *Is Latin America Turning Protestant?* Berkeley, CA: University of California Press.

Teixeira, F. *et al.* (1993), *CEBs: Cidadania e Modernidade*, São Paulo: Paulinas.

Tennekes, H. (1985), *El Movimiento Pentecostal en la Sociedad Chilena*, Iquique: CIREN.

Van Dijk, R. (1996), 'From Camp to Encompassment: Discourses of Trans-subjectivity in the Ghanaian Pentecostal Diaspora', *Journal of Religion in Africa*, XXVI (4), pp. 1–25.

Walls, A. (1990), 'The Translation Principle in Christian History' in *Of the Church*, Leiden: Brill, pp. 24–39.

Walls, A. (1992), 'The Western Discovery of Non-Western Christian Art' in Wood, D. (ed.), *The Church and the Arts*, Oxford: Blackwell, pp. 571–85.

Walls, A. (1995), 'Christianity in the non-Western World: A Study in the Serial Nature of Christian Expansion', *Studies in World Christianity*, 1 (1), pp. 1–25.

Waters, M. (1995), *Globalization*, London: Routledge.

Chapter Seven

CONVERSION AS NOSTALGIA: SOME EXPERIENCES OF ISLAM

Tim Winter

Together with Christianity and Buddhism, Islam is in theory and in its historical habit one of the world's foremost missionary religions. Were it not for the Koranic commandment to 'arise and warn', the youngest of the major global faiths might have remained the sect of a few obscure Arabian monotheists, destined to fade away as the peninsula slowly acceded to the vibrant Christianity which surrounded it. Instead, in a manner which remains puzzling to those historians who seek to reduce history to a narrative of economics and society, the backwater of Mecca engendered a great kerygmatic movement powerful enough to overwhelm the political order in the more prosperous and advanced civilizations which it encountered, and also, still more remarkably, to transform a deeply entrenched religious order which by the usual laws of acculturation would normally have assimilated its conquerors. Fourteen centuries after the death of its founder, Islam continues to exercise an appeal in a remarkably wide variety of societies. It is hence surprising that while the religion's proselytizing temper is one of the most significant constants of world history, it is still only inadequately understood.

In seeking to make sense of this complex and resilient dynamic, the present study progresses through three areas of enquiry. First, a few introductory remarks will be offered on what the phenomenon Christians call 'conversion' has meant in an Islamic scriptural and theological context. Second, the most conspicuous episodes of conversion in Islamic history will be outlined, accompanied by a synopsis of the prevailing scholarly interpretations. Finally I advance some necessarily tentative speculations about the new phenomenon of Internet 'cyberconversions', as a sample area in which to test the present validity of established theoretical models of conversion to Islam, and of the conversion phenomenon more generally.

First, of course, comes the theology. Since its inception, the religion of the Prophet Muhammad (*c.* 570–632) has sought to multiply the ranks of the faithful; its founding document, the Koran, is a recital of God that is also a summons. Lamenting the idolatry of Mecca and its tribal hinterland, the Koran's reformism is more drastic even than that of Jesus of Nazareth six centuries before, since whereas Christ's Jewish audience had been monotheistic, and was hence not categorically to be denounced, Muhammad's audience appeared to the Koran to have no redeeming features whatsoever. The Muslim scripture does not urge a refinement or culmination of the religious views which supply its immediate historical context; it rejects them unconditionally. The primitive Islamic ethos is hence insistently polemical and conversion-oriented. The climax of the Prophet's ministry, the sermon at the Mount of Mercy, ended with Islam's equivalent of the Great Commission: 'Let those who are present convey these truths to those who are not.'[1]

Despite this initial *sitz im leben*, the sources available to us do not believe that the Prophet restricted his ministry to the heathen Arabs. As recalled and constructed by the Muslim memory, Muhammad was not sent only 'to the lost sheep of the children of Ishmael'; he was, as a hadith announces, 'sent to all mankind'; indeed, the medieval schoolmen of Islam consensually held that Islam is the only divinely purposed universal religion. Jesus, on this classical Muslim view, believed his mission to be solely to the Jews, so that Christianity's subsequent Gentile mission was providential only as a kind of *preparatio evangelii* which broke the pagan ground in readiness for Islam. Far from constructing a particularist Arab salvation history, as some modern historians have suggested, the Koran is remarkably uninterested in the Arab people, never once extolling it as the bearer of a particularly momentous past or destiny. Although rabbinical Judaism was the most accessible monotheism to the religion's founding milieu, Islam is not a rewriting of Judaism for a fellow Semitic people. If attempts to reconstruct the temper of the Prophet's mission are at all reliable (and all but the most radical of modern historians accept that they are), then there is abundant evidence to show that from an early time the Islamic dispensation was emphatically universal in its ambition. Several of the Prophet's most intimate disciples and apostles were of non-Arabian stock: the tradition preserves the names of Suhayb the Greek, Salman the Persian, and Bilal the Abyssinian, the first muezzin of Islam.

Despite this context of outreach, the Koranic lexicon includes no terms for 'conversion'. This is because the Arabic word *islam* itself entirely incorporates the concept. The word is the verbal noun of a causative form of a root connoting 'safety', 'salvation' and 'peace'. Hence to enter Islam – in the active participle, to become *muslim* – is to place oneself within the pale of God's saving activity. As a loving God (*al-Wadud*), the Creator wishes success in the next world for all humanity. The Koran urges: 'Enter into deliverance (*silm*), altogether' (2:208), and: 'Whomsoever God wishes to guide, He opens his breast to *islam*' (6:125). Hence the Koranic notion of conversion to the righteous life is not one of sudden rupture, but implies that the *muslim* will live in a dynamic state of experiencing and striving to merit a lifelong process of conversion to God. There is no Muslim equivalent of being 'in Christ', of thereby receiving an assurance of salvation, because for Muslims soteriology hinges not on the sacrifice of an atoning Saviour, but on the struggle of the faithful soul to purge itself of distraction and to experience grace directly. Hence one of the most consistent features of Muslim conversion narratives is gradualism, coupled to a consequent assumption of open-endedness. Traditional words spoken to the new proselyte are: 'You have won the battle; now you must fight it.' The 'born again' or psychotropic type of conversion is comparatively unusual, as most modern converts report a slow process of assimilation and mimesis, in which rational proof is perceived as playing a major role.[2]

A further aspect of the Koranic soteriology which underpins this specifically Muslim idiom of 'conversion', or *islam*, must also be understood. *Islam* is conventionally less dramatic, and less affective, than an Augustinian *conversio*, since it does not understand the history of human salvation as a titanic confrontation between a God whose realm is heaven and the spirit, and the devil who prevails on earth and in the flesh. Islam has no concept of original sin, since the Koranic God fully 'relents' towards Adam. It has, by contrast, a doctrine akin to what Matthew Fox calls 'original blessing',[3] and denies the belief that creation is radically separated from God. The human creature is itself innately possessed of grace, so that according to a hadith, 'every child is born with the true natural disposition (*fitra*), it is only its parents that turn it into a Jew, a Christian, or a Zoroastrian'. This doctrine is presumed from Koran 7:172, which refers to the Great Covenant (*mithaq*) when all souls, before being disseminated into the world, were called before God to witness. The passage speaks of a time

> when your Lord brought forth from the Children of Adam, from their loins, their seed, and made them testify of themselves. He said: 'Am I not your Lord?' They said, 'Yea, we testify!' That was lest you should say on the Day of Resurrection: 'Of this we were unaware'.

The Sufi poet Rumi (d. 1273) is entirely conventional within this tradition when he describes his sense of conversion to God:

> Before this [life], the spirits were upon the spheres, drinking
>   from the same cup as the angels.
> My spirit is clapping its hands, since Thou art pulling it back
>   to the same place.[4]

Convinced of the indicativity of nature, and of the fundamental innocence of the soul, Islam seeks to do no more than remind humanity of this primordial witnessing to and of God. Conversion, *islam*, is a remembering (*dhikr*); it is a turning-in and an affirmation, not a denial of what one already is. For this reason, the great majority of new Muslims today refer to themselves as 'reverts', not converts. 'Recognizers' might be still more accurate. The usual idiom in Spanish is *reconocerse musulmán*: to recognize oneself as Muslim.

Motivated by this simple and distinctly optimistic view of human nature and the religious life, the first Muslims scattered as victorious conquerors over the ancient world. There followed one of the most bizarre episodes of religious history, as the bulk of the countries of the Church Fathers experienced the only mass apostasy recorded in the career of any of the monotheisms. Patriarchal centres such as Alexandria, Antioch and Jerusalem, where Christianity had slowly taken root several centuries earlier, acceded gradually but permanently to the new religion. As the leading historian of the process remarks: 'Most of the descendants of most of the men and women who, in the year 600, believed that Jesus of Nazareth was the Son of God now profess a belief in Allah and in Muhammad as his messenger.'[5]

The city of Gaza presents a typical case. The Christianization of this city had progressed only slowly, and yet, on the arrival of the Arab conquerors,

> the Gazan people responded with alacrity to the call to convert to
> the new religion . . . and they asked, according to local historians,
> that the great church in the centre of the city be converted into a
> mosque . . . Not all Christians agreed to convert to Islam when
> the Arabs arrived; and they were given the right to worship in
> the church of Porphyry (built in 442) – which still occupies the
> same site near the centre of Gaza city.[6]

There is insufficient space here to try to arbitrate between the sharply debated interpretations placed on this process. The following generally accepted findings must, however, be noted. First, since the publication of Sir Thomas Arnold's work *The Preaching of*

Islam in 1896,[7] it has been acknowledged that the conversion of most of Christendom to Islam was not coercive, but voluntary. Hence one modern historian of Muslim Spain records that 'historians are virtually unanimous in saying that there was neither proselytizing nor persecution of Christians by their Muslim conquerors'.[8] Second, since the appearance in 1950 of D. C. Dennett's *Conversion and Poll Tax in Early Islam*,[9] historians have discarded the earlier view that most conversions took place to escape discriminatory taxation levied on non-Muslim subjects of the caliphs. The rates of taxation do not appear to have been high, and in many cases were not suspended upon conversion. Thirdly, Richard Bulliet's 1979 monograph *Conversion to Islam in the Medieval Period* showed that most conversions took place not in the immediate aftermath of the conquest, but in the three or four centuries which followed, which Bulliet calls the 'Age of Conversions'.[10] Hence we now believe that Egypt and North Africa became majority Muslim countries sometime in the mid-ninth century; Iran, slightly earlier; while the Iberian peninsula was at least four-fifths Muslim by the beginning of the twelfth century. These three discoveries support the general conclusion of Levtzion, writing in 1979, that 'military conquest was not necessarily followed by widespread conversion', but that it appears a century or so later,[11] a pattern confirmed by studies of the Islamization process in areas conquered by Muslim dynasties in the later medieval period, such as North India, Anatolia and the Balkans.

Levtzion and Bulliet, and the field generally, record that although they ostentatiously based their claims to legitimacy on religion, Muslim polities almost never actively sought the conversion of their minorities. Conversion to Islam was typically the consequence not of official pressure, or of an alleged collapse in indigenous Christian or other institutions, but of increasing social interaction between Muslims and non-Muslims. Partly out of a desire to consolidate Islam's hold on the Arabian tribal levies, the early conquerors had held themselves aloof in military cantonments, and only when these had evolved into major urban centres which could attract a steady influx of indigenous migrants from the hinterlands did extensive contact between the conquerors and conquered become possible. The conversion process thus began slowly, and accelerated steadily, as new converts themselves became points of contact with the unenlightened masses.

With the close of the Age of Conversions in the eleventh or twelfth century, the Islamization of the remnant unconverted populations proceeded much more slowly, and was usually the work of two overlapping social groups. The first of these comprised itinerant merchants whose association with the world's dominant civilization gave their creed and manner of life great prestige in the eyes of their customers. The second group was composed of peripatetic Sufi mystics and saints who attracted unbelievers by their working of miracles and cures, by their willingness to write and sing in vernacular languages, by their frequent willingness to allow processes of gradual transition, and by their advocacy of an appealing love relationship with the divine. The conversion of Anatolia, Bosnia, Kashmir, Indonesia, and regions of West Africa, was largely made possible by Islam's ability to nurture these two inherently mobile and dialogical forms of piety: the mercantile and the mystical.

Sufi mystics, in particular, were the instrument of Islamization in the subcontinent of India, where the Bulliet model appears to apply only irregularly. The first three centuries following Islamic incursions into India witnessed few conversions; and a Middle Eastern acceleration never really took hold, possibly because of the greater conceptual gulf which lay between Islam and Hinduism, and perhaps also owing to the greater stratification and modularization of Hindu society, which allowed it to retain its coherence and its religious credibility even when the ultimate political power was no longer in Hindu hands. However, the theses of Arnold and Dennett are amply confirmed by the Indian experience inasmuch as it has been shown by Richard Eaton and others that the conversion of Hindus was often more common beyond the frontiers of Muslim rule in India than in the Muslim-ruled areas.[12] The expansion of Muslim political hegemony, and the growth in adherence to the Muslim religion (here usually among the lower castes), appear to have been two largely separate processes. Contact with Muslim advocates was the usual trigger for conversion, not the policies of faraway sultans.

Further east, the Islamization of the Indonesian archipelago, which was not subject to armed Muslim invasion, appears to offer further confirmation of the encounter thesis. The close-knit populations of Hindu India were only infiltrated by Islam over a period of many centuries, so that even today, Muslims number only around a third of the subcontinent's population. By contrast, Java, Malaya and Sumatra, although also largely within the Indic cultural orbit, offered less resistance, so that today over 90 per cent of Indonesia's population is Muslim. The reason appears to be that the division of the region into several thousand populated islands facilitated Muslim access, given Islamic domination of the maritime trade routes.[13]

In all the regions of Islamic proselytization, a pattern is hence discernible. First, purely missionary institutions were lacking: while the Sufi orders may frequently have acted as cultural mediators, they were not founded with mission to unbelievers as their main objective. Second, the overwhelming majority of conversions appear to have been voluntary. Third, Islamization tended to be gradual, frequently involving a prior acculturation to Islamic values through encounter with Muslims, or with partially Islamized elements, and hence a process of what A. D. Nock refers to as 'adhesion'.[14]

It is clear, however, that although the encounter and adhesion models are persuasive as a sociological framework, they fail to disclose the explicit motivation of the individual human subjects. The fact of Muslim social interaction with others does not in itself constitute an explanation for conversion on such a scale. The puzzle is, moreover, made still more difficult by the existence of a range of deterrents which rendered the Muslim option less obviously enticing to potential proselytes.

One of these deterrents took the form of the social disadvantages which could accrue from conversion. While an ambitious migrant to a growing city like medieval Damascus or Baghdad might be tempted to adopt Islam for the sake of social mobility, he or she could expect severe isolation from the community of origin, given that pre-modern Christian and Hindu groups typically regarded apostasy as an act of treason entailing automatic outcaste status. As though to symbolize this, Islamic law provided a further disincentive by denying converts to Islam the right to inherit from their unbelieving parents. For most medieval converts, the advantages conferred by joining a community often hardly outweighed the problems raised by leaving one.

A second enigma is supplied by the demanding nature of Islam's religious expectations. However profound his ignorance might otherwise have been, an eighth-century Syrian peasant or trader contemplating conversion would have known that this step would entail the painful rite of circumcision. St Paul had facilitated that peasant's ancestors' conversion to Christianity by declaring that the old Abrahamic rite was now supplanted for all who were 'in Christ'. Islam, however, did not make this concession.

Another potential intimidation offered to the prospective convert was the religion's ritual system. Islam requires five daily acts of worship, the first to be offered well before sunrise. It also expects participation in the Ramadan fast, an onerous duty in hot climates. It urges the payment of an obligatory annual tithe to the poor, usually equivalent to one-fortieth of one's wealth. It imposes the duty of the pilgrimage to Mecca, itself an expensive, uncomfortable and, in medieval times, hazardous undertaking. The religion also imposes dietary restrictions unknown to Christians, of which the prohibition on eating pork is only the most obvious. It forbids the consumption of alcohol, allowable to non-Muslims by Islamic law.

In addressing this apparent conundrum of Islam's success, one way forward may be to recall the nature and origins of the religion itself. As already noted, the Koran emerged as the argument of a marginalized and persecuted sect against an oppressive order. As a body of scripture, the Koran and the Prophetic-sayings literature which supplements it, constitute a discourse of conversion that deliberately speaks to a particular human psychology. The Koran consoles the early Muslims with assurances that their marginality will be shortlived: 'And it is Our purpose to show favour unto those who are oppressed in the earth, and to make them leaders, and to make them the inheritors' (28:5).

Given this 'liberative' tenor of the Koranic discourse and of the Prophetic biography, it is unsurprising that Islam should historically have appealed to marginal communities. Today, in the United States, black converts outnumber their white co-religionists by a factor of twenty to one. The population of the early medieval Near East, often sharply alienated from the Greek-speaking clerical and political élite of Byzantium, and then from the succeeding Arab kingdom, may have responded in a similar way. The Christian subjects were marginalized, although not oppressed by the state, and may have sought relief in the state's own religion, which, although now empowered, originated as a discourse of consolation and promise. There may also have been a related element of defiance. Recent conversions to Islam among the scheduled castes in India have been understood by at least one sociologist as a 'strategy for protest'.[15] Protest conversions are a recognized phenomenon for sociologists of religion, having been documented most exhaustively by Irwin Scheiner in his book *Christian Converts and Social Protest in Meiji Japan*, which documents how samurai who had lost their social status as a result of the Meiji Restoration adopted Protestantism as a sign of protest.[16]

Islam's emergence as a kind of liberation theology which offered an accessible language of protest against social marginalization is hence one credible factor in its success. Another is the appeal of the religion's concept of God. Islam taught a simple monotheism which appealed to many who had been confused by christological and trinitarian controversies, rapidly putting down roots in many territories such as Egypt and Spain which preserved strong memories of the Arian and related debates. The Muslim conviction that ultimate reality must be ultimately simple persuaded not only the peasantry, but also clergymen such as Theodisclus, St Isidore's

successor as Archbishop of Seville, who had apparently held adop-
tionist beliefs before finding a resolution of his difficulties in
Islam.[17] This is what Lamartine had in mind when he described
Islam as

> practical and contemplative theism. The sort of men who believe
> in it cannot be converted: one moves from a dogmatic system full
> of miracles toward a simpler kind of dogma, not the other way
> around.[18]

Finally, it is also clear that the world's oldest and most profoundly
Christian communities would not have peaceably acceded to Islam
had its advocates not demonstrated a strong and impressive religious charisma, and a palpable holiness of life.

It is far from clear whether such classical models of conversion to
Islam have much contemporary relevance. It is uncontroversial
that the religion continues to experience numerical growth:
Samuel Huntington suggests that the Muslim proportion of the
globe's population has increased from 12.4 per cent in 1900, to
around 20 per cent at the end of the twentieth century, and will
reach an estimated 30 per cent in 2025.[19] However this expansion
is overwhelmingly the result of natural increase in the largely
Third World communities where Muslims live. There exist no reliable statistics to disclose the extent and nature of the missionary
reach of modern Islam.

There is no doubt, however, that the traditionally Christian
countries of the West are now experiencing patterns of Islamization.
The most demographically prominent instance is the African-
American Muslim community, numbering today in the region of
four million, whose accession to Islam, represented and reinforced
by celebrity converts such as boxer Muhammad Ali and the rights
activist Malcolm X, can readily be interpreted as a movement of
protest against centuries of maltreatment by white Christians. The
process has been facilitated by the diffusion of Muslim themes in
such forms of popular black culture as rap music, and also by the
rise of syncretistic movements such as the Nation of Islam which,
by instituting such concessions as allowing mosque congregations
to sit on chairs rather than on carpets, function as stepping-stones
from a Christian to a Muslim identity.[20] Thus understood, this
major transformation of the modern American religious landscape
appears to validate two of the theories of conversion to Islam outlined previously: that of the protest from the social margin, and the
theory of gradual adhesion.

More difficult to interpret is the far smaller but no less persistent pattern of conversions among more privileged ethnic groups. Many accessions to Islam in modern Europe and America take place among the white majority, although even here Islam's perceived 'preferential option for the poor' figures regularly in motivations, as in the case of Roger Garaudy, the former chairman of the French Communist Party who converted in 1981,[21] or the ballet choreographer Maurice Béjart, for whom Islam is part of a third-worldist and anti-colonialist stance.[22] However, by no means all in-dividuals who convert from privileged backgrounds show an expli-cit interest in making a gesture of protest, and partly for this reason this movement has attracted the attention of several recent re-searchers.[23] The number of white converts is not considerable (perhaps fifty thousand in the UK, and a hundred thousand in France); but to the extent that the world as a whole is progressively being reshaped in the West's image it is believed that this phenom-enon may indicate the future idiom of conversion to Islam on a more global level.

One of the most visible areas of activity for these converts is the Internet. This most complex of all human artefacts is a formless Tower of Babel where the established religions, including Islam, are generally on the defensive. Nonetheless, there are signs that the Internet is serving as a new point of contact between Muslims and others, enabling a missionary advocacy which allows us another vantage point from which to examine conventional theories of Isla-mization. Among Muslim diaspora communities in the West, the Internet has already become a retardant to familiar processes of ac-culturation to the values of the host communities. Websites allow isolated Muslims in the remotest parts of America or Australia to order books and prayer beads, locate prospective spouses, listen to sermons via audio links, and to discuss their concerns, via electronic mail, with an indefinite number of other Muslims. This total aboli-tion of geography, once the most immutable factor in the diffusion of culture, throws into serious question conventional sociological theories about the assimilation of immigrant and other minority groups. The scale of the phenomenon is already considerable: the website of the Islamic Society of North America (www.islamici-ty.org) recorded almost twenty million 'hits' in the two years up to February 1999, and aims for a target of one billion by the second decade of the new century.

This same elimination of distance is beginning to wield a major influence on the conversion process. A farmer in Idaho is no longer limited in his knowledge of non-Christian religions by the stock at his county library. With a little 'surfing', unimpeded and unembar-rassed by face-to-face contact with advocates, he can anonymously log on to computerized concordances of the Koran and Hadith, read polemical literature against Christianity, and, with patience, construct a reasonably accurate picture of the religion as it is held by the majority of technically literate Muslims.

Inevitably, a new phenomenon has made its appearance: the internet convert, or 'cyberconvert'. Many Islamic websites founded by cradle Muslims cater for this individual. For instance, the website of the Belfast Islamic Centre includes a brief guide to Islamic worship for new Muslims.[24] There is a 'Non-Muslim Page', which debunks 'stereotypes', and offers a toll-free number for religiously minded web-surfers who wish to know more about Islam.[25] A British site dishes out videos with the boast that 'We have converted many people to Islam, both males and females, and from a variety of different religious and social backgrounds.'[26] In America, there is an Online Islamic Propagation Team, which describes itself as

> an online community of Muslims aimed at spreading Islam via web pages, email, chat, message boards and news groups ... Muslims should be active in spreading Islam among the users of the cyber world.[27]

An anti-Christian site includes video footage of a Muslim debating with the American evangelist Jimmy Swaggart.[28] Another offers the text of a book on the Bible by a Uniate Catholic bishop who converted to Islam,[29] while a site in Brazil supplies similar material in Portuguese.[30] The Edmonton Islamic Resources page discusses a selection of 'convert issues', and gives advice on 'An Islamic Alternative to Christmas'.[31]

In addition to these sites operated by immigrant groups, there are websites run by the converts themselves. Some of these are introspective and lack a clear missionary orientation. For instance, six sites run by the Murabitun World Movement, a British-based organization which claims several thousand converts in various countries, is clearly a discussion platform for group members, with little interest in outreach.[32] There is a homepage run by and for women converts, which again is confined to discussions and pastoral advice for new arrivals.[33] The majority of convert websites are, however, clearly proselytizing in intent. Some are specialized, like the Hispanic Muslims Pags, by definition a convert page, administered by Puerto Ricans,[34] or the site of the Muslim Converts Association of Singapore.[35] The majority of Spanish websites appear to be run by converts, hardly surprising given the domination of Islamic organizations in Spain by these latter-day descendants of the Moriscos. Hence, the secretary-general of the state-recognized Islamic Direc-

torate, a Madrid brain surgeon who is also a convert, runs the Direc-
torate's very sophisticated web magazine.[36] A sub-page is dedicated
to material on Islam in Catalan.[37] For these highly motivated neo-
Muslims, the Internet opens new horizons for missionary work.

A recurrent feature of the convert sites which links them to the religion's past missionary experience is their interest in Sufism, an
aspect of traditional Islam which cradle Muslims in the West frequently appear to disregard. These sites are too many to list, but,
to take a few examples, there is the *Giardino della Cognoscenza* site in
Italy, run by converts to the traditionally conversion-oriented
Naqshbandi order, which is clearly designed to attract non-
Muslim 'seekers'.[38] Virtual visitors are invited to discover more
about the Naqshbandi order by visiting its lodges, and addresses
are provided of many dozens of these.[39] The site guides readers to
another Italian site, operated by converts to the Jerrahi order, origi-
nating in seventeenth-century Istanbul but now claiming several
thousand converts in the West. The Jerrahi site offers a portrait
and a brief biography of the spiritual leader of the Jerrahis in Italy:
the visitor learns that he is a painter and lecturer in psychology at
Milan University, is shown his photograph, and is invited to consider his aphorisms on the spiritual life.[40] The international 'seeker' is
then directed to the site of the Jerrahi Order of America, which
gives details of the humanitarian and relief work which is traditional
in the order, and lists addresses of more Jerrahi lodges in Bosnia,
Germany, Greece, France, Austria, Canada, Spain, Mexico, Argentina and Brazil.[41]

This phenomenon of the cybertariqa, the Sufi order whose
members are widely dispersed but who remain in touch electronically, must be seen as one of the most remarkable developments in
the history of Islamic mysticism. Cybertariqas foster a sense of community among far-flung group members, disseminate the teaching
of the group leader, and also develop the Sufi tradition of seeking
new acolytes. Hence the Western seeker can now dispense with
voyages of discovery to the East, and can simply tap into the websites of most of the thirty or so orders active in Western countries.
Prospective members unable to visit the spiritual guide can follow
his discourses electronically, buy his books, and observe major gatherings in mosques, lodges and conference centres.

On the fringe of this luxuriant Sufi missionary activity there exist
other cybertariqas which do not perceive themselves as Muslim,
but which fold together elements of Sufi teaching with New Age
beliefs and practices. The patron saint of these groups is the Persian
mystic Rumi, currently the best-selling religious poet in America.
The historical Rumi was a devout thirteenth-century Muslim

scholar, but in his selective, syncretistic New Age guise he has been transformed into one of the liberal gurus of the Internet. In this way the Western spiritual seeker can log on to 'flute music inspired by Rumi', or join a discussion group for those who appreciate his poetry, or view Rumi-inspired digital artworks.[42] The non-Muslim 'Sufi Order of the West', which draws much of its inspiration from Rumi, invites seekers to join the 'Electronic Sufi Class', where in complete anonymity they can learn religious techniques designed to complement rather than challenge their existing affiliations.[43]

Some *tariqas* include both Muslim and non-Muslim members. One of the most successful of these is the Bawa Muhaiyadeen Fellowship of Philadelphia. Founded by a Tamil saint and anchorite of Sri Lanka, this movement has outlived its founder's death in 1986, partly by the skilful use of the Internet. The guests of its eirenic and aesthetically perfect website are informed that, in the Sufi tradition, visitors to the Fellowship mosque in a wealthy Philadelphia suburb will receive a free vegetarian meal; an ideal opportunity, no doubt, for attracting new membership.[44]

By such techniques a continuum is established which allows the Western 'seeker' to identify with a Sufi group without, in the first instance, harbouring the least idea of accepting Islam. This leads to greater familiarity with the religion's ambient culture, the adoption of certain rituals and beliefs, and often, in due season, to formal conversion. As in the case of the Black Muslims, this pattern falls in neatly with Nock's adhesion thesis, where new systems of worship are accepted at first as auxiliary rather than as replacement practices, with the definitive break with the old religion following later.

To summarize a very complex picture, it appears that Muslim proselytism on the Web occurs in two main contexts: first, sites run by immigrant Muslim organizations attempting to win converts, frequently by adopting an abrasive approach to Christianity, and second, sites run by converts, which are typically oriented towards Sufism, and which initiate seekers into the religion through a series of innocuous and gradual steps, including the use of technology to bring the teacher's charisma to potential acolytes.

To attempt to impose some form of academic order on these involved processes, and to discern how, if at all, traditional processes of Islamization as identified by Bulliet and others are still operative in this new medium, a prototypical experiment of a rather simple nature has been attempted. This was carried out by analysing a sample of 100 convert testimonials culled from as wide a variety of websites as possible. Such an approach cannot yield exact results, since the type of convert who enthusiastically bares his soul to the world is not necessarily normative. The absence of an interviewer or questionnaire may lead to the inconsistent reporting of factors commonly considered to be major aspects of the conversion process, such as parental divorce or alcoholism. Moreover, the websites themselves may suppress information about certain types of conversion which conflict with their doctrinal line. Despite this, however, certain cautious conclusions can be drawn which appear to cast significant light on the traditional theories of Islamic conversion.

These 100 converts constitute a very heterogenous group. Around three-quarters are American, from a wide spectrum of socio-economic classes. Exactly 50 are women, suggesting a reappraisal of the commonly reported view that women account for around three-quarters of Western converts.[45] The age distribution of the converts does not differ significantly from that of the general population. Between 80 and 90 of the subjects have converted since 1993. Only two attributed their conversion to an experience of a Muslim country. Five were former Christian missionaries. Six were conservative Catholics unhappy with liberal theology and vernacular liturgy. Fifteen had already left Christianity due to doubts over the doctrine of the Trinity, while eight specify disillusionment with the concept of original sin. Three were former Jews, and four others report having considered converting to Judaism. Three were Chinese, eight, perhaps more, were African-Americans, and three were Native Americans. Seven, and probably more, converted following marriage to a Muslim. Six report conversions following dream or visionary experiences. Twenty-nine report that reading the Koran was the catalyst for their conversion.

One of the most recurrent themes is the sense of having taken a step which appears gentle and obvious to the subject himself ('as easy as eating a slice of pecan pie' as one convert put it), but which is momentous and problematic in the eyes of family, acquaintances and the wider society. Particularly in the United States, conversion to Islam is not a socially acceptable event. Since the Iranian hostage crisis in 1979 negative perceptions of Muslims have been rising steadily, so that according to a recent Roper opinion poll, over half of respondents in the US describe Islam as 'inherently anti-American', while in 1997, the Council on American–Islam Relations reported an increase of 60 per cent in cases of discrimination.[46] The opprobrium which attaches to an Islamic identity appears central to the concerns of the great majority of the American converts, who consistently report hostility and forms of harassment. One example, from the testimony of the daughter of a Baptist minister in a small Bible Belt town, indicates the nature of the problem:

I returned home one afternoon . . . to find that someone had shot at the windows of my home, and spray painted 'TERRORIST LOVER' down the side of one of my vehicles. The police were no help to me at all. That same night while chatting to Muslims on the Internet, I heard gunshots ring out. They had returned, and finished almost all the remaining windows that were left in my home, and killed my pets that were outside.[47]

The same convert goes on to describe a physical assault which left her hospitalized, followed by a series of other interventions by hitherto affable neighbours. She claims not to be disheartened, however, since although she lives over a hundred miles from the nearest mosque, 'what little knowledge I have about Islam has been gained through reading everything I can find on the internet, and through my true friends and family on the web'.

Other converts also report extreme scenes of rejection by family and by local communities. The sample includes accounts of missionary parents who became convinced that their convert offspring was possessed, and of other parents who called the police, believing conversion to Islam to be an offence.

Given this adversarial attitude to Islam, which recalls the communal counter-pressures applied against converts in the medieval Middle East, conventional theories of adhesion appear problematic. Ironically, however, it appears that the same attitude supplies a leading factor in the conversion process. A frequent feature of the testimonies is the statement that the initial desire to learn about Islam was triggered by extreme dislike, and a desire to convert Muslims. For instance, one former Catholic seminarian felt, as he records:

that these Muslim nations must be destroyed . . . I knew that I would do my duty by converting Muslims to the Christian faith . . . But after a couple of years of debate with the Muslims and researching the topics in all the Holy Books, I embraced Islam.[48]

Another American spent his teenage years listening to 'prophecy experts' on fundamentalist radio stations. As he recalls: 'Their paranoid espousal of various conspiracy theories, rabid support of Israel and religious Zionism, and fiery preaching about the 'Islamic threat', held for me a strange fascination.' His curiosity developed as follows:

I began to visit the religion folders on AOL and the Usenet newsgroups, where I found discussions on Islam to be the most intriguing. [I learnt] that Muslims were not the bloodthirsty, barbaric terrorists that news media and the televangelists paint them to be.[49]

His stereotypes duly shattered, he contacted a local mosque, and was accepted into Islam.

A lapsed Fransciscan priest tells the following story:

> One night I was watching the news on television, and of course they were continuing their one-sided half-truth reports on Muslims. I decided to research Islam for myself and draw my own conclusions. What I found was the opposite of the negative images that the satanic media spewed forth. I found a religion deep in love and spiritual truth, and constant God-mindedness.[50]

Eight out of the total hundred record that negative media images of Islam triggered the curiosity which led to their conversion. This corresponds to the experience of Mustafa Tougui, the official responsible for conversions at the Puits d'Hermitage mosque in Paris, who believes that a majority of educated French converts enter the faith 'ironically', having begun their trajectories with a curiosity aroused by negative media portrayals of Islam.[51]

The odd conclusion must hence be drawn that conversions may accelerate during periods of strong anti-Muslim sentiment, with the Internet facilitating this process by allowing direct access to communities. Although further research would be needed to demonstrate this, to correlate the dates of, for instance, episodes of violence against Muslims with an increase in the posting of conversion testimonies on the Web, the hypothesis may be regarded as reasonable. It certainly appears to challenge the view of Levtzion, writing of the Age of Conversions, that 'success is Islam's advertisement'.[52] More generally, it allows us to conclude that the Internet is an evolving context and conduit for a style of conversion which transcends socially constructed counter-pressures. It also continues and adapts another ancient theme, that of the protest gesture, drawing on the strong tendency in modern politically correct culture to desire solidarity with misrepresented communities, and to 'challenge stereotypes'.

The phenomenon of Internet conversions hence suggests that classical patterns of recruitment to Islam continue to be operative in this modern, or even post-modern, environment. Themes such as the importance of encounter (which is the Web's pre-eminent gift), the marginal or protest conversion, processes of gradual adhesion, the disillusionment with trinitarian discourse, and the attraction of Islamic mysticism, appear to be no less efficient today than in the medieval past. Whether Islam's history of growth through conversion can maintain itself, however, may depend not solely on these time-honoured channels of transformation, but, more fundamentally, on the ability of an endlessly mobile modernity and the inherently conservative Islamic ethos to continue to find grounds for some mutual comprehension, and hence to provide a terrain of communication for Islam's mediators. Whether such an outcome becomes a reality will have major implications for the religious future of the world.

Notes

1   Muhammad al-Bukhari, *al-Jami' al-Sahih* (Cairo, 1313 AH), Hajj, p. 132.
2   This is noted by the two most careful modern studies: Larry Poston, *Islamic Da'wah in the West: Muslim Missionary Activity and the Dynamics of Conversion to Islam* (New York, 1992); and Ali Köse, *Conversion to Islam: A Study of Native British Converts* (London and New York, 1996). The prevalence of gradual processes of conversion is also remarked upon by Lisbeth Rocher and Fatima Cherqaoui, *D'une foi à l'autre: les conversions à l'Islam en occident* (Paris, 1986), p. 21; and also Marcia Hermansen, 'Roads to Mecca: Conversion Narratives of European and Euro-American Muslims', *The Muslim World*, 89 (1999), pp. 79–80. Early Anglo-Muslim converts also remarked upon the easiness of the transition: see Nabil Matar, *Islam in Britain, 1558–1685* (Cambridge, 1998), pp. 21–49.
3   Matthew Fox, *Original Blessing: A Primer in Creation Spirituality* (Santa Fe, NM, 1983).
4   William Chittick, *The Sufi Path of Love* (Albany, 1983), p. 70.
5   Richard Bulliet, 'Process and Status in Conversion and Continuity' in Michael Gervers and Ramzi Jibran Bikhazi (eds), *Conversion and Continuity: Indigenous Christian Communities in Islamic Lands, Eighth to Eighteenth Centuries* (Toronto, 1990), p. 2.
6   Gerald Butt, *Life at the Crossroads: A History of Gaza* (Nicosia, 1995), pp. 78–9.
7   Sir Thomas Arnold, *The Preaching of Islam: A History of the Propagation of the Muslim Faith* (Westminster, 1896). An earlier but less widely noted expression of this thesis was given by the Anglo-Muslim convert Abdallah Quilliam in his *The Religion of the Sword: An Enquiry into the Tenets and History of Judaism, Christianity and Islam, with a view of considering which Religion has been the most Tolerant* (Vol 1, Liverpool, 1891).
8   J. McWilliam, 'The Context of Spanish Adoptionism' in Gervers and Bikhazi, *Conversion and Continuity*, p. 76.
9   Cambridge, MA, 1950.
10 Richard Bulliet, *Conversion to Islam in the Medieval Period: An Essay in Quantitative History* (Cambridge MA, 1979).
11 Nehemia Levtzion (ed.), *Conversion to Islam* (New York, 1979), p. 9.

12 Richard M. Eaton, 'Approaches to the Study of Conversion to Islam in India' in *Approaches to Islam in Religious Studies*, ed. Richard C. Martin (Tucson, 1985), pp. 106–23.

13 Marshall G. S. Hodgson, *The Venture of Islam* (Chicago and London, 1974), Vol. II, pp. 542–51.

14 A. D. Nock, *Conversion: The Old and the New in Religion from Alexander the Great to Augustine of Hippo* (Oxford, 1933), p. 7.

15 Abdul Malik Mujahid, *Conversion to Islam: Untouchables' Strategy for Protest in India* (Chambersburg, 1989).

16 Irwin Scheiner, *Christian Converts and Social Protest in Meiji Japan* (Berkeley, 1970).

17 Arnold, *The Preaching of Islam*, p. 136.

18 Cited in Hisham Djaït, *Europe and Islam: Cultures and Modernity* (Berkeley and London, 1985), p. 31.

19 Samuel Huntington, *The Clash of Civilizations and the Remaking of World Order* (New York, 1996), pp. 65–6.

20 Nuri Tinaz, 'The Nation of Islam: Historical Evolution and Transformation of the Movement', *Journal of Muslim Minority Affairs* (1996), pp. 193–209.

21 Rocher and Cherqaoui, *D'une foi à l'autre*, pp. 16–17; R. Garaudy, *Mon tour du siècle en solitaire: Mémoires* (Paris, 1989).

22 Rocher and Cherqaoui, *D'une foi à l'autre*, p. 127.

23 See note 2 above. There is also a considerable literature generated within the Muslim community. Representative are Salim Admad *et al.*, *Into the Light* (London, n.d.), and the anonymously edited *Islam Our Choice* (London, 1983 and many reprints). Much information is also provided in the regular *Meeting Point: the Newsletter of the New Muslims' Project* published by the Leicester-based Islamic Foundation.

24 ireland.iol.ie/ ~ afifi/Articles/mukallaf.htm

25 www.geocities.com/Athens/6810/nmp.html

26 home.virtual-pc.com/wipecrc/wipeinfo.htm

27 members. aol.com/IslamTeam

28 www.users.globalnet.co.uk/ ~ iidc/iidci_frames.html

29 www.mosque.com/goodialg.html

30 AvSete.fst.com.br/ ~ sbmrjbr/alah.wav

31 syed.afternet.com/index2.htm.convert

32 Listed at www.geocities.com/Athens/Delphi/6588/index.html

33 members.aol.com/Samiyha/muslimah.html

34 members.aol.com/Samiyha/hispmuslim.html

35 www.darul-arqam.org.sg

36 www.verdeislam.com

37 www.webislam.com/tx_97_04.htm

38 www.geocities.com/Athens/Delphi/5291

39 www.naqshbandi.org

40 www.geocities.com/Athens/4044

41 www.cco.caltech.edu/ ~ kzehra/joa/who.html

42 www.egnet.co.uk/clients/music/tbh.html; www.Rassouli.com/Rumi.
    htm; www.onelist.com/viewarchive.cgi?listname=ruminations
43 www.sufiorder.org/eclass.html
44 www.bmf.org.
45 Lucy Berrington, 'Secure in Sisterhood', *The Times*, 9 November 1993.
    For women converts see Carol N. Anway, *Daughters of Another Path: Ex-
    periences of American Women Choosing Islam* (New York, 1995); Harfiyah
    Ball, *Why British Women Embrace Islam* (Leicester, 1987); Laleh
    Bakhtiar, *Sufi Women of America: Angels in the Making* (Chicago, 1996).
46 www.usnews.com/usnews.com/usnews/issue/980720/20isla.htm;   see
    also www.cair.com
47 www.algonet.se/~ulwur/reverts/amirah.htm
48 www.algonet.se/~ulwur/reverts/jim.htm
49 www.usc.edu/dept/MSA/newmuslims/yahiye.html
50 www.cadvision.com/ybernier/david.htm
51 Adam Le Bor, *A Heart Turned East: Among the Muslims of Europe and
    America* (London, 1996), p. 164.
52 Levtzion, *Conversion to Islam*, p. 12.

Chapter Eight

CONVERTING AWAY
FROM CHRISTIANITY

Andrew Wingate

Conversion out of Christianity to another world faith is a highly contextual question, depending not just on theological questions which themselves may well be locally influenced, but also by all kinds of psychological, social, political and historical factors. I look at modern South India and why individuals and groups who have converted to Christianity, often at great cost, revert to Hinduism, or convert actively to Islam. I am concerned with these three religions which are the predominant ones in South India. Hindus represent about 90 per cent of the population of the four southern states, Tamilnadu, Kerala, Andhra Pradesh and Karnataka, and Christians and Muslims about 5 per cent each. I concentrate on Tamilnadu, a state with a population about equal to Britain, where the religious proportions are approximately as above. I taught at the Tamilnadu Theological Seminary, Madurai, and what I write below comes out of living experience and research.

The largest Christian church in Tamilnadu is the Roman Catholic Church, followed by the Church of South India, several Lutheran Churches, and numerous independent and Pentecostal Churches. The mainline churches are products of the missionary movements of the last three centuries and they have long been under Indian leadership. Conversion to Christianity was normally in community movements, where a group of families or a whole village decided to convert. The majority of such conversions were from Dalit groups (so-called 'untouchables', also known as Scheduled Castes) and those who came from other castes were usually also poor. The same did not apply to individuals, and there were many prominent conversions of high-caste people who often suffered deeply for the decision they made.

During colonial times it was an advantage for a poor community to become Christian. There was a real hope of liberation from the chains of casteism and of bettering themselves by education in church schools and other means. This is not to discount the very real spiritual experiences often involved which led an individual to take a lead in encouraging a group to convert. Inevitably there was also a sense of joining a 'Western' religion, which appeared to be the way the future was going. But, since 1947, and increasingly in recent years, Christianity has ceased to be such an attractive option. Christian Dalit converts lose a number of benefits available to Hindu Dalits and, however hard the churches have agitated, no government, local or national, has given Christians the same deal as their Hindu counterparts. These benefits relate especially to higher education and employment in the large state sector. There has also arisen a climate where it is felt by many that to be Indian means to be Hindu. Extreme Hindus have tried to change the constitution to make conversion illegal. This has been particularly so through the Bharatiya Janata Party (BJP), which recently formed the national government, and brought great pressure on Christians. As I write, this government has just fallen. But any government, even one led by the Congress Party with its secular ideology, these days needs to take account of the vital Hindu votes, and cannot afford to be betraying the major religion of the country.

Conversion to Islam

But there has also been the phenomenon of group conversion from Christianity to Islam, and I begin with this. This can be paralleled within the African Continent and elsewhere, as groups, villages and tribes move between these two world religions. Such changes have deep political implications. The population balance between faiths has political dimensions in many places and India is one of them. In recent years the most famous such example in India is Meenaakshipuram, where in 1981 fifteen hundred persons converted to Islam in the Tirunelveli District of Tamilnadu. This became a national issue and every effort was made by Government and Hindu organizations to stem the tide and to win re-conversions. Of those who converted nearly all came from one Dalit caste known as the Pallars. They are the 'highest' of the main three Dalit sub-castes in the area and hence are not the poorest of the poor. Educationally and economically they have made some progress and many are small landowners. But what they can never do is lose their untouchable status in Hindu eyes and the daily petty oppression they suffer from the Shudra castes just above them. Islam provides the possibility, especially for the young, of acceptance into a religion where they will be treated as brothers and receive protection from harassment. Much as an attempt was made to prove that petro-dollars were used to induce conversion, no evidence was found by researchers or the government; these other reasons were sufficient explanation in themselves.[1]

In total, Muslims estimate ten thousand conversions in Madurai and Ramnad areas in the post-Meenaakshipuram period, very important symbolically even though a small number within the population of Tamilnadu, yet alone India. A small proportion of these converts were Christians. I next consider a village where Christians became Muslims, in which I spent a considerable amount of time over several months and with which I have kept in touch since.

This village named Kanday is of the same caste as Meenaakshipuram and the news of the conversions there had spread widely. Conversion began with two villagers, who had met Islam when they went to work outside, asking some Muslims to come and share their faith. I was present to hear a Muslim preaching and at a later 'kalimah' conversion ceremony. Emphasized were the solidarity of old and new Muslims, the breaking down of untouchability symbolized in the sharing of food at the celebratory meal (each took a handful of cooked food and placed it on the plate of the neighbour) and a simple theology based on the oneness of God and the need to give up idol worship immediately. They were warned not to expect Gulf money, but to stand on their own feet.

In Kanday most families have fertile land and this gives them a strong sense of self-worth. They proudly say they have never been bonded labourers. The Pallars dominate the village, but when they step outside they face much petty harassment which is a continual insult to their dignity. The first Christian conversions here were in 1919 and the history of the church was not without problems – relapses, deaths reported as due to the revenge of the Hindu God, a school established and then closed, varied pastoral support, the sense that they were neglected by the outside church. The congregation leader I met in 1981 said he rang the bell every Friday and Sunday. I saw that he read the service from an almanac of 1965. Tiles were beginning to fall off the roof and the communion vessels were smeared with dirt. No pastor had been for 18 months. That year, only four families had paid the Christmas festival 'tax', while there had been 40 at the peak. Some had gone back to Hinduism, others had gone to Islam.

The Mullah for the Muslim converts in the village was a new convert. His wife was an old Muslim and they were a living witness that such marriages are possible. Teaching was given after admission, not before, when the desire to be a Muslim was enough. Prayer and practice were given more importance than doctrine or theology. A few basic points were stressed repeatedly, the Mullah teaching the men, his wife the women. Several youths were sent outside for further training. I heard the children reciting the Qur'an in Arabic as happens anywhere in the world.

I met many individuals, of whom there is space here to detail only two typical examples. Mohammed Sultan grew tired of casteism in the community and church. He instanced that the only higher-caste Christian family in the vicinity would not allow Dalits into their home. He wanted to make improvements for his children, if not for himself. He had witnessed the funeral of a new Muslim else-where and the respect shown pushed him to invite Muslims to come to the village. His wife found things less easy, he admitted, but she had to accept. But equality remained at the centre and he quoted the high-profile marriage of a new Muslim to the daughter of a rich Muslim businessman. Another new Muslim said, 'The English converted us and left us, but Muslim brothers are here and can defend us. If you want us to worship as Christians, take us to England!' He was impressed with Muslims in worship, where king and servant sit next to each other. Jesus' dream of one flock and one shepherd had been fulfilled in Islam.

The local high-caste Christian mentioned above confirmed this attitude to me, admitting her way with Pallars was not like that of Jesus in the Gospels – but he had no weddings to arrange! She would visit them to pray and mix with them in church; they should not expect more in Christianity, and they were welcome to go to Islam if it would better them.

I visited again in 1994 and 1997 and found that there had been a further decline in the Christian congregation, with just a couple of families holding on, and, to my great sadness, the church building in a very poor state. I saw for myself the strength of the Muslim com-munity, which has a strong leadership. The Imam even took me to meet the Christian families, suggesting I encourage them and say prayers with them! The Hindu community has also revived, and it is Christianity that has almost gone.

J. Aruldoss, a lecturer from Madurai, has organized a regular vis-iting programme since 1992 in local districts where there are new Muslims. He comments,

In the context of caste oppression in India, particularly in Tamil-nadu, Islam is seen as a liberative religion by the Dalits and con-tinues to convert even now. According to their experience, they believe that Islam annihilates the problem of untouchability to a certain extent and changes their identity from the so-called un-touchables to Muslims. It also provides a different world view, hope and new life for them. They feel that they are accepted into a community where the spirit of corporateness is still alive.

As we have seen, it was from amongst the more prosperous Pallar community that conversion to Islam took place. They could more afford to take risks. Their economic position was not matched by their social status; education had raised their expectations for social acceptance and this hope had not been realized through joining a secular movement, with none of the main parties, including Marxist ones, matching practice to preaching in support of Dalits.

A further local factor is the peculiar character of Tamil Islam. Mattison Miles substantiates what I have observed.[2] His studies show that, of all the Muslims in India, Tamil Muslims practise least a system of social stratification that can be likened to the Hindu caste system (this may seem strange when Tamil Hindus are particularly wedded to the system). This does not mean there are no social divisions, but they are relatively less sharp. Moreover, converts continue to use the same language and share the same culture as their neighbours.

Press publicity about the Meenaakshipuram conversions was enormous and, since these Christian Pallars had a high level of education, this meant handbills could be read, leading to the question, 'If others converted, why not us?'

A non-aggressive but strategic evangelism emphasized the discipline of Islam, its worship, the oneness of God, with Jesus as well as Muhammad being his prophets, practical outcomes of teaching in terms of cleanliness of life and an end to bad habits. Narrow religious experience was not central, nor indeed expected, rather submission to a new way of life, with an emphasis on social justice.

Important was residence of an Imam in the village and the support shown by influential Muslims from local towns. They provided role models of success, particularly in business; some offered employment but this does not seem frequent. But the new converts were also encouraged to live in harmony with their neighbours and relatives, enabling more conversions within extended families. Women usually followed men and the subordinate status of women was nothing new to village women.

Further factors relate to experience of the church. There was an absence of local leadership and ineffective pastoral work. Knowledge of these village Christians was low, belief abstract, and worship largely non-participatory. The community was divided on personality and caste grounds both locally and amongst church authorities. Above all, there remained a dependency, with expectations raised by the missionary days and present-day pastors being unable to offer what is required.[3] The result is an educated but depressed community who are a ready target for Muslim evangelism.

Reversion/Re-conversion to Hinduism

Hinduism is not a religion which seeks converts from non-Indian communities. There are modern-day exceptions, such as the Hare Krishna movement, and various guru-led sects. But mainstream Hinduism is concerned with Indians. There is a desire amongst more militant Hindus to 're-convert' Indians who have entered other faiths. In this section we consider this movement. At the same time we look at the experience of 'reversion'. This indicates a general drift back to Hinduism which happens by slippage and neglect, as Christian practice gradually ceases and the old takes over. The parallel in the Western context would be the active churchgoing Christian who gradually ceases practice, first by not going each week and then each month and finally not even at Christmas and Easter. Here the drift is normally to the predominant secularism of the society around. In India it would normally be to the Hinduism around. In both societies, there may be no catalyst, just apathy, other priorities or a sense of disappointment with the Church. In the West there may be a conscious turning away from belief, or a feeling that there is no longer a need for God. This is not normally the case in India, where religious faith is the norm.

Active re-conversion as a result of a conscious decision involves taking part in a specific ceremony. This may be a response to energetic evangelical Hinduism, led by such organizations as the Arya Samaj, founded in 1875 by Swami Dayananda. In South India Christians have become a target, particularly in the last two decades. Economic advantage is now in becoming Hindu again. Appeal can be made to Indian nationalism and to the sense that they have not escaped from the caste system in Christianity.

The re-conversion movement is known as 'suddhi', the name also given to the ceremony marking this. This is basically a purification ceremony, more obviously necessary with caste Hindus who have become polluted by contact with outsiders. So-called 'untouchables' were polluting before and remain polluting afterwards. Details of the full rite are given in a study by J. F. Seunarine.[4] After re-conversion, another important event is the publication of the old (Christian) and new Hindu name in the Government Gazette. Nothing could make clearer that such conversions are political as well as religious, and this sits at variance with the constitutional position of India as a secular state. When a Hindu converts to

Christianity or Islam nothing is recorded, giving the appearance that traffic is all one way (like those who convert to Catholicism from the Church of England in modern-day Britain). The convert now has a new status and can apply for reserved work or a scholarship.

What will be clear from the following case studies is that re-conversion takes place for a number of reasons, but that loss of faith in Christ is not normally one of them. When I asked one of the groups questions in belief terms they did not know what I was talking about. If you belonged to a Christian community, you worshipped Jesus; if you changed your community, then you worshipped the appropriate god of that community. Moreover, there would be nothing to stop you continuing to worship Jesus in your heart and even to put up his picture alongside Hindu gods.

The reason why many follow one religion rather than another is what they receive from it. If the Christian community does not provide protection, dignity, acceptance and material progress, then its members may seek these elsewhere. Acceptance is vital, whether from pastor or fellow members of the Church. Worship, too, is critical as a unifying factor. If it takes place regularly and the people feel part of it, other things follow. If it happens rarely, and they do not feel they belong, then rapidly they begin to reabsorb the prevailing Hindu culture. Little by little they join in the festivals and weekly puja. They may begin just by eating at festivals and stop there. But their children may go further, particularly if they marry Hindus. Before long, it just becomes a memory: 'Our family was once Christian.' The giving of Hindu rather than Christian names to children is an important step in this process, as names signify so much in this culture.

By way of example, I write of three individuals. The first took his family back to Hinduism because, as a low-caste Dalit, he was asked to sit at the side of the church when an important speaker came. His thinking was, 'Caste is part of Hinduism, but we expect respect in the church.' As that was not forthcoming, he returned to his old faith to secure a better future for his children. My second example is a youth with a degree, one of several I met, who, after college, was three years unemployed. He made the decision to reconvert without telling his family, since they would have opposed and considered him 'unclean'. But the ceremony which involved bowing to what he felt was an idol gave him great guilt. He obtained work in a government bank, but at great psychological cost. He now tries to persuade other unemployed Christians not to follow him.

My third example is a young man whose story is easy to parallel with that of isolated youth in any place throughout the world. As a rebel, he rejected his family Christian religion and, when he went to work in Madras, felt like a puppet hanging loosely with no one to pull the strings. Perhaps there will be an increasing number of such young people in cities, the product of the urbanization of India and the loss of the stable values. He now drifts in and out of Hindu temples and cults.

I now consider group reversion. As an active step on a particular day by joint decision this is a fairly rare phenomenon, though I did study two such examples, one caused by pressure from Hindu extremists, the other by church division and caste conflict. Much more common is a gradual drift, and we will examine a typical example of this.

In Veryapur, caste divisions are strong between high-caste landlords and Dalits. Conflicts are frequent, and liberation for the landless is far away. Suppressed economically, socially and religiously, it is not surprising that there was a move towards Christianity between the wars. The church expanded rapidly and the pastor in the 1950s had forty villages to look after. He had two evangelists and, for transport, a bicycle.

A generation after conversion, caste relations were not bad, with Dalits being able to wear sandals and drink from the same tumblers. The villagers are vague about when they became Christian, but remember the pastor involved. The critical issue was pastoral care, and in recent years this had begun to slip. In 1981 there were three active Christian families out of the original forty-five and the smaller children had Hindu names, the older ones Christian.

An old retired Bible woman came occasionally to teach the children. She was not respected by the adults and was no substitute for a pastor. No catechist had visited for four years and the house was let for rent. The present pastor had only called twice, visiting only those who attended the church, not 'backsliders'. The majority now went to Hindu temples, though some of the relapsed went to church at Christmas. The church leader had struggled to hold things together, leading the worship on the basis of one month's training twenty years before. He felt unsupported by the pastors. The problem of pastors not visiting is less serious in the 'decent' villages, but the 'lower' villages suffer. These villages need weekly worship and regular visiting if they are to remain faithful. The Government officer had been and offered loans. Twenty-five people who are Christian gave Hindu names to get help – Daniel gave Karuppan, Moses Yeliyan, Asirvatham Puttan.

Only one of the group had been confirmed and there was a certain vagueness even as to what it is. A number had joined groups such as the Christian Fellowship Church and the Full Gospel Young Men's

Association, who evangelized, using Indian music. They would like to use Indian culture more in the church, but the authorities had sold the instruments. They borrowed from the Hindus to use at Christmas time.

Such villages are very tender plants. Conversion happened for various reasons: relative connections, marriages, expectations for economic development, need for social dignity or protection, food aid. The latter aims were normally fulfilled in early years, but Christianity did not become rooted enough to mean it remained firm when these benefits were no longer on offer. Nevertheless, where adequate ministerial structures were established, storms could be weathered. This is indicated by the regularity with which certain pastors' and catechists' names are mentioned as being willing to share their lives. Where such support was absent, the prognosis was poor and decline quite rapid. Within ten years we seem to be left with occasional observance for some centred around Christmas, Christian-Hindu practice by others and full Hindu relapse by a third group. Others join sectarian groups, where 'spiritual experiences' are encountered, strikingly absent in stories coming from these villages.

It tends to be the poorest villages which revert. They have high economic expectations because they possess very little. Such questions should be recognized honestly before baptism – can what they hope for explicitly or implicitly be fulfilled, not only in the short but the longer term? Moreover, they have very few representatives amongst the ordained ministry.[5]

What draws people to Hinduism, where are the 'pull' factors? A strong message increasingly being broadcast in the media is that the Church is a Western import. A pamphlet, for example, suggested that Christians will hand back the country to England and Muslims sell it to Arabia. Alongside these political factors goes the call to return to the traditional ways of the village, which is where one's karma leads one. People may have a sense of guilt that they have laid aside the Hindu practices which had sustained their parents and grandparents and, under pressure, these things come to consciousness. Moreover, the pluralism of Hinduism means that it is easy to return to Hinduism and still hang a picture of Jesus in the house, along with Hindu gods. Not much will be demanded by Hinduism, nor will the ethical demands be great. Positively, there is the attraction of the annual round of festivals, lacking in non-Roman Catholic churches. Some recent forms of Hinduism also suggest it can be casteless, as witnessed by photographs in the press of large demonstration intercaste meals.

At the family level, the pressure to conform at 'good and bad' times in life will push one back, as well as the dishonour of belonging to a split family. The difficulty of finding a Christian partner from the same caste background makes marriage a likely time for individual reversion. Family pressure also affects the educated young pulled to re-convert for employment possibilities.

Where are the 'push' factors out of Christianity? First on the list come caste-related issues. Conversion to Christianity had been expected to bring liberation from caste since in Christ there is no slave nor free. Yet though there is normally equality in worship, this often does not continue outside the church building. Dalits, in particular, feel they have no power, nor possibility of marriage outside their subcastes. What they perceive is as important as statistical reality. Such caste discrimination may be experienced in general, or as a result of particular incidents. And those who are not Dalits are perceived as polluted by joining a beef-eating and 'low' religion.

The 'pull' of Government job reservations and educational scholarships is significant for the educated. The potential loss of these did not seem greatly to hinder conversion to Christianity, at least up to the 1980s. Converts were either ignorant of this and kept ignorant, or they were coolie workers or small farmers for whom these concessions had been of no practical help. But with later generations, as they become educated through Christian schools, the frustration of unemployment for educated youth is powerful in pushing some to reversion. The 'pull' element will be obvious when Hindu youth of the same or lesser educated status are more easily gaining employment.

To compensate, the church may be expected to provide unlimited employment. This may be through schools, projects, hospitals, administration, Christian businesses, or ordained ministry. Failure to obtain such employment can lead to dissatisfaction and lay the seed for a drift from active church membership. So also does the end of economic benefits, such as gifts of wheat or rice. Another cause of dissatisfaction is the feeling that others, including Hindus, are given places in Christian educational establishments, rather than deserving Christian children.

At the congregational level, lack of effective teaching, ineffective worship, the appointment of a pastor who is not one of their caste and who appears to look down on them, or family quarrels may push them towards re-conversion.

At the individual level, moving from the village to the city for work or education may be the catalyst. Their confidence may recede, and reverting to the past may be an easy option. Some individuals have experienced healing as a cause of conversion and, if

sickness returns, reversion may follow. Actual loss of belief appears
to be rare. From time to time and perhaps in an increasing way
under Western influence, strongest when they migrate to cities,
people lose their belief in God.

Even when several of the above 'push' and 'pull' factors are
present it is not inevitable that there is a move away from Christianity. Loyalty to one's decision can be very strong and this is often a
real loyalty to Christ, if not to the Church. It is so often the figure
and experience of Christ which converts and that is not easily re-
versed, even if social and economic advantage is towards reversion.
There may be a fear of the guilt involved if one attended a Hindu
temple and thereby rejected Christ. There may be a fear of evil
spirits/the devil avenging for such apostasy.

Family pressure may be an obstacle in well-established Christian
families, where there is a wish to remain loyal to traditions. There
may be contempt for village Hinduism as superstition and idol-
worship and as a primitive faith. Classical Hinduism may well be
seen as Brahminic and oppressive, Islam even more foreign than
Christianity, while Buddhism is almost unknown in Tamil villages.
Therefore it is preferable to stay where one is.

Conclusion

Conversion to Christianity happens for many reasons, but the most
important, my research shows, relate to an experience of liberation,
and this is often incarnated in belonging to a community on the
way to freedom.[6] Through the love a convert experiences, or positive involvement with a local congregation, he or she finds a community which reveals the Body of Christ, and the liberating God of
which they hear in the Bible. This may be a religious experience of
liberation and acceptance, but also may include a move towards
social and economic freedom. Such conversion is a process, and is
always open to reverse. What is perhaps surprising is that most
Indian Christians do not revert under the pressures to which they
are subjected, showing much about the depth of their religious
rooting. Being in hardship together is bearable where there is good
leadership, a strong sense of solidarity, and a clear understanding
of faith expressed in regular inclusive worship which encourages a
deepening of commitment to Christ. What is clearly different from
the past two hundred years or more is that the missionary zeal of
Christianity is being matched and might even be overtaken by the
missionary strategy in Islam and in evangelical Hinduism – hence
the need to strengthen the church members as a community of faith.

The key question remains for an Indian Christian, where can we find a liberated life? Or at least, as liberated as possible within our realities? Where is the truth that will 'make us free'? Is it to be found by remaining in Christianity with its clear ideology of equality? If not, is it there within Islam, which does not seek security in government concessions, but in the solidarity of the 'umma' (community of Islam)? Or do disappointments mean converts feel they will be as well in their own village Hindu traditions, where at least they are not under any illusions as to their place, and this thought leads to reversion?

Notes

1 Writing and research about Meenaakshipuram has been extensive. See Mumtas Ali Khan, *Mass Conversion of Meenaakshipuram* (Madras: CLS, 1983); and the whole volume of *Religion and Society*, XXVIII (4) (December 1981), including my extensive study of two Christian villages which converted to Islam.

2 Mattison Miles, 'Muslim Stratification in India' in *S. W. Journal of Anthropology*, 28 (1972), pp. 333–49, and 'Islamisation and Muslim Ethnicity in South India' in *Man* (NS) 10, pp. 404–19, reprinted as 'Social Stratification among Tamil Muslims in Tamil Nadu' in Imitiaz Ahmed (ed.), *Caste and Social Stratification among Muslims in India* (Delhi: Manohar, 1973). For a very recent study of Indian Muslims, cf. Mushirul Hasan, *Legacy of a Divided Nation; India's Muslims since Independence* (Delhi: Thompson, 1997).

3 See my book *The Church and Conversion* (Delhi: ISPCK, 1977), and particularly Chapter 9, on ministry to the converted.

4 J. F. Seunarine, *Reconversion to Hinduism* (Madras: CLS, 1977).

5 This was a big issue in the neighbouring Tiruchi Diocese, where for a number of years in the 1970s, most from the caste broke away from the CSI (see unpublished MTh thesis of J. Dorairaj, Tamilnadu Theological Seminary).

6 See again my book *The Church and Conversion*.

Chapter Nine

CHRISTIAN CONVERSION 1900–2000: WILLIAM JAMES TO LEWIS RAMBO

Timothy Yates

Introduction

From the beginning of the Christian movement, conversion has been an important phenomenon. The early preaching seems to have included the call to individuals to 'turn from idols to serve the living and true God' (1 Thessalonians 1.9) and what was true of Paul as a missionary to pagan Greeks has continued as an emphasis among missionaries and evangelists since his time. The New Testament leads us to believe that baptism followed for those who did turn. By this means, individual converts were made members of the Christian Church as a visible corporate body. Modern missionaries have often been anxious to assure themselves of the reality of the inner turning of the heart before agreeing to give the outward recognition of baptism: to assess the willingness of the convert to forsake the old in order to embrace the new, at often great personal cost. To depart from the faith of the ancestors and the social and cultural moorings of traditional life among primal peoples was to risk alienation. There are numerous accounts in modern missionary history of individuals who have faced persecution and expulsion from their communities and families. In what follows, three twentieth-century treatments of conversion are examined, all three addressed to the psychology of Christian conversion and one of them, that of the French scholar Raoul Allier, specifically arising from experiences of conversion in primal mission fields. All three cast light on the often complex psychological processes which we label as Christian conversion.

Such Christian conversion has its roots in the New Testament era, with the earliest accounts being given by Luke in Acts, those of Saul of Tarsus (given three times by Luke, presumably to emphasize its importance), Cornelius (given twice), the Ethiopian treasurer and eunuch, Lydia and the keeper of the jail at Philippi. In the cases of Saul and the jailer these are specifically conversions to the risen Christ and calls to action. So Saul asks, 'Who are you, Lord?', and the reply is, 'I am Jesus, whom you are persecuting ... enter the city, and you will be told what you are to do' (Acts 9.5–6 NRSV). The jailer asks 'What must I do to be saved?' and receives the answer, 'Believe on the Lord Jesus, and you will be saved, you and your household' (Acts 16.30–1 NRSV). Cornelius is urged by Peter to trust in the crucified and risen Christ in order to receive the forgiveness of sins. While the idea of turning or returning to the Lord was common in the Old Testament (the verb transliterated *shub* has 1,050 occurrences) and is taken up in 39 uses of the verb *epistrephein* in the New Testament, as also in the use of *metanoein* in the preaching of John the Baptist and Jesus, describing in both cases a change of mind of direction and allied in Jesus' preaching to a call to recognize the advent of God's kingdom (Kittel 1965, pp. 722–9), what differentiates Christian conversion is that the turning is towards the person of Christ. So Lesslie Newbigin defined it as 'the inner turning of the heart and will to Christ'; but in so doing he is anxious to show that, as in the initial experience of Jesus' disciples in his earthly ministry, there remain three constituents to the experience:

1 a personal relation to him;
2 a visible community;
3 a pattern of behaviour.

'The inner turning of the heart and will', he wrote, 'must neither be separated from, nor identified with, membership in the visible community and commitment to the pattern of behaviour.' The call to repentance and faith is a call to 'turn round in order to participate in this new reality', that is, the Kingdom of God, and is 'a commitment to action' (Newbigin 1969, p. 147f).

William James

While the New Testament showed little interest in the psychology of conversion, with the emphasis, as Newbigin pointed out, on *action* rather than on *experience*, the three twentieth-century treatments here have all focused on this latter aspect. William James was a philosopher who taught at Harvard. He was elder brother of the novelist Henry James. They were sons of a father who had been strongly influenced by the Swedish theosophist, Swedenborg. William James belonged to the school known as 'pragmatism', which has

been defined as 'the doctrine that the test of the value of any assertion lies in its practical consequences' (Drabble 1985, p. 452). This
gave him a natural interest in conversion, for conversion may be
thought to provide empirical evidence that ideas have identifiable
effects. In his work *Pragmatism* of 1907, James argued that 'true
ideas are those that can be corroborated and verified ... an idea is
made true by events'.

The work by which William James is best remembered is his *Varieties of Religious Experience* of 1902, the Gifford lectures given at Edinburgh. The ninth and tenth lectures are specifically devoted to
conversion, although the rest of the book has a good deal of material
which relates to it. His treatment has been fairly criticized as highly
individualistic.

James's case studies are of individuals in North American or
European contexts and relate to their personal experiences. There
is little here of the second constituent noted by Lesslie Newbigin as
essential to Christian conversion, relationship to the visible community, although changes in behaviour get due recognition. James's
distinction between the 'once born' and the 'twice born', which he
borrowed from F. W. Newman, has attracted theological criticism:
it is held, properly enough, that the New Testament looks for new
birth for all, of which baptism is a sign. 'The distinction made by
William James between once born and twice born Christians is a
pretty epigram but poor theology. The NT knows only twice born
Christians' (Parker 1982, p. 75). Perhaps, however, there is some
continuing validity in the phrase as it is used to distinguish between
what are often called 'cradle Christians' and, for example, adult
converts, who have sometimes become Christians after considerable
mental and psychological turmoil. James's examples are of less interest to missiologists than our next writer's, in so far as they are examples of those in a Christian culture 'coming alive' to the
Christian message after many generations of a society's exposure to
it, rather than a transfer of allegiance from an alternative cultural
and religious *Weltanschauung*.

The Unified Self

James defines conversion in a frequently quoted sentence:

> To be converted, to be regenerate, to receive grace, to experience
> religion, to give an assurance are so many phrases which
> describe the process, gradual or sudden, by which a self hitherto
> divided and consciously wrong and unhappy, becomes unified

and consciously right, superior and happy, in consequence of its firmer hold upon religious realities. (James 1977, p. 189)

In commenting on this, E. Stanley Jones was closer to our original definition in changing the last phrase from 'religious realities' to 'a person': 'the religious realities are a Person' and 'the divided life is "unified" around a new centre, Christ' (Jones 1960, p. 47). The aspect of the divided self, to which James devoted his eighth lecture, will recur later: he pointed to Augustine, Bunyan and Tolstoy as examples. The unification of the self

> may come gradually or it may occur abruptly ... however it comes brings a characteristic sort of relief ... Happiness! Happiness! Religion is only one of the ways in which individuals gain that gift. Easily, peacefully and successfully it often transforms the most intolerable misery into the profoundest and most enduring happiness. (James 1977, p. 175)

Tolstoy is given as an example of a gradual return over the years to the faith of his childhood, but his experience gave renewed 'energy' (Tolstoy's choice of word) in common with other experiences recorded by James. James wrote: 'The personality is changed, the man is born again' and there is a 'new level of spiritual vitality ... and new energies' (p. 241). He gives also examples of sudden conversions, those of the eighteenth-century Christian Henry Alline of Boston and the nineteenth-century French Jew from Paris, Alphonse Ratisbonne, and others to show what a 'real, definite and memorable experience and event a sudden conversion can be', one in which often the subject seems to be 'a passive spectator ... of an astounding process performed upon him from above' (pp. 223, 226).

James does not only use 'above' language himself. He recognized that much of conversion may be subliminal: 'the notion of a subliminal self' ought not either to 'exclude all notion of a higher penetration. If there be higher powers able to impress us they may get access to us only through the subliminal door' (p. 243). Like our next writer, James was aware of the often strange accompaniments to both conversion and revival, the influence of dreams and what one of the authorities he quotes refers to as 'the possession of an active subliminal self' (pp. 240–1). James concludes on this aspect: 'If the grace of God miraculously operates, it probably operates through the subliminal door' (p. 270).

James realized that psychology, of itself, is unable to give an account of the source of conversion or even why those aims which have primarily been peripheral become for the object, in his phrase, 'the habitual centre of his personal energy' (p. 196). He himself leaves the door open to a spiritual interpretation in a conclusion which may owe something to his father's Swedenborgian views: 'The visible world is part of a more spiritual, from which it draws its chief significance' and 'Union or harmonious relation with that higher universe is our true end' (p. 486). He also recognized that, for the convert or mystic, their experiences can be 'absolutely authoritative in the individuals to whom they come' (p. 422). To take one prominent twentieth-century Christian, well known to missiologists, who confessed himself sorry for the 'once born' of William James's classification, Stephen Neill:

> For those who can look back on some recognisable experience of conversion in their own lives this is so much more important than anything else that they find it very difficult to take seriously any type of Christian living from which this experience is eliminated ... I have not the smallest doubt that through conversion I became a new man in Christ and that it was literally true that all things became new in Him. (Neill 1950, p. 352).

Raoul Allier

The second of our twentieth-century authorities on conversion is of great interest to students of mission. Raoul Allier, who wrote as a professor in the University of Paris, published his *La Psychologie de la conversion chez les peuples non-civilisés* in 1925. He wrote in his preface that it was during a previous project on moral evil that he stumbled on the periodical of the Société des Missions de Paris called the *Journal des Missions Évangéliques*. This discovery in 1888 fired his imagination with the potential of missionary accounts for an exploration of conversion. In addition to the journal mentioned, he used a number of others, including the *Bulletin de la Mission Romande* (the Swiss Mission) and the *Journal de l'Unité des Frères* (Moravian). He came, he wrote, to the whole study 'entirely disinterested' and had originally intended to include Roman Catholic missions, but decided that the differences of operation were such that it would be better to limit himself to Protestants. Nevertheless, his examples came from a very wide range of fields including Madagascar, New Guinea, Greenland, Central and East Africa, the New Hebrides, Tahiti and Fiji. He used the printed reports of the great missionaries of the Paris Evangelical Mission, François Coillard, Maurice Leenhardt and Hermann Dieterlen and the equally great missionary and renowned anthropologist, Henri Junod, of the Swiss Romande Mission: but did not confine himself to French sources, and accounts from Johannes Warneck among the Bataks and a CMS missionary like Richard Taylor among the Maoris also feature. He was acquainted with the anthropological writings of Lévy-Bruhl and with the psychology of Sigmund Freud, including his work on dreams. The work was in two volumes, the first of which divided into two parts 'Les Prodromes de la Crise' and 'La Crise' – 'prodromes' appears to originate with the Greek and Latin words (*prodromos, -us*) for a north-east wind which promises a change in weather conditions and can perhaps be translated 'stirrings' or 'winds of change'. His second volume, which will not be handled here, was entitled 'Les Conséquences de la Crise' and the whole, with its treatment of over a thousand pages, must rank as one of the most extensive enquiries into conversion ever undertaken.

'Hardening', Sorrow and Dreams

In the first part of Volume I, Allier shows how resistant to conversion many individuals could be. One chief tells Coillard, 'The law of God is hard, difficult', and another tells a Moravian missionary in Greenland, 'We could have no objection to conversion if it were not so difficult.' King Sekhone of the Mangorato tribe told the Scottish missionary Mackenzie: 'For me to accept the way of God is as if I wished alone to attack ... all the hordes of the Matabele' (Allier 1925, pp. 131–2). Debased and debauched habits cause a Tahitian to describe himself as 'in chains', language, writes Allier, 'which is universal' for describing moral experience (p. 149). There is a clear recognition that the issue of conversion lies in the realm of the will: a chief asks Johannes Warneck, 'Where will I find riches and power if I never make war nor have slaves?' (p. 141).

Maurice Leenhardt produced a new slant on this resistance, what Allier calls 'endurcissement', or hardening against change. He found that it was possible to judge the spiritual position of his hearers by the allure of horses as a means of physical escape from the demands of his message: in one case, a man took himself off at a gallop, in another he retreated to another part of the same valley which had not yet been Christianized (pp. 201, 202). Malagasy parents went to the extent of hiding their infants in 'silos' to escape missionary detection. One African spoke for many in the various fields when he said to the missionary: 'You speak well but my heart is not ready'; or, with a touching faith in the missionary's prayers, as one of Warneck's hearers said: 'You ask God who is perhaps able to change me; I am not yet ready' (pp. 203, 213).

As with William James's accounts, there is pain, or what Allier calls 'visible sorrow', before conversion: one woman, Mapati, reported on by Hermann Dieterlen, moves from tears to joy (pp. 328–9). The occurrence of pain and even illness prior to conversion causes Allier to compare the phenomenon with stories recorded of Huguenots in the seventeenth century who became ill after renouncing their allegiance under political pressure. Allier judged that the deep distress before conversion was made up both of the *pain of converting* and, quite as much, of the *pain of not converting*: there was both a sense of an *obligation to change* and a *sense of responsibility for being in a permanent state which was condemned* (pp. 328–30). He compared it to Paul's heartfelt expression in Romans 7.19–23. What is at issue is a new 'I', a new identity. In a section which he entitles 'The two me's' he finds universal use of the language of the 'two hearts' by Maoris, New Caledonian Kanaks and Zambezi Africans. Moshesh, the Lesotho chief, said to Robert Moffat: 'Before I listened to you I had only one heart, now today I have two.' Allier also gives an interesting example of subliminal factors at work: an African under the influence of chloroform speaks as if he was a Christian believer, although in waking life he is known not yet to be a Christian (pp. 351, 365–6). A Malagasy who appears to speak with the voice of the persecuting Queen Ranavalona I and associated ancestors gave evidence, as he did, that 'the old "me" repulses what it sees as a menace' (p. 364).

This led Allier to devote an extensive section to the place of dreams as a factor in conversion, along with hallucinations and 'voices'. Of the first he wrote: 'The number of conversions provoked by dreams is incalculable.' Unlike Western missionaries (but not unlike William James, as we have noticed), his subjects are not trained in mind to discount the power of a dream to provoke major change in life. Hermann Dieterlen, at first very reluctant to accept dreams as in any way a source of the divine, admitted that 'it is possible it is not absolutely wrong'; that is, God may have influenced the converts through dreams (pp. 373–4).

A typical example is of the chief who dreams that he is in the forest and wishes that Christians should pray for him to dispose of his fetishes: this chief, Kasi Ahang of Akropong, was so moved by his dream that he acted upon it (pp. 380–1). Allier commented on this and other examples: 'It would appear that the moral will, vanquished during waking hours, takes its revenge during sleep: it is the new "me" which emerges victorious' (p. 377). Reports of such dreams come from many fields: Kils, Malagasies, Kanaks, Africans from the Congo, Negroes from Surinam (Dutch Guiana) (p. 374). In some cases dreams seem to have prepared the way for the acceptance of the gospel, as appears to have been the case in Nicaragua before the missionaries' arrival or, less spectacularly, in Nias, where an elderly priestess believed that she had been instructed in a dream by the ancestors to pronounce in favour of the new religion (p. 370). We shall return to the place of dreams in the conclusion of this paper.

Death and Rebirth

Allier's treatment of the experience of conversion itself, 'La Crise', makes reference early on to William James. Like James, Allier described conversion as a new release but also as a form of death to reach that point. The call, as given by the missionary Withney to the Malagasies, was to 'abandon yourselves'; but such self-abandonment, Allier recognized, was 'in a certain sense a form of death' (p. 435). One Malagasy convert, at first powerless to respond to such a call, then described himself: 'I feel myself as revived from the dead.' Henri Junod had noticed how often converts used the formula 'I have been conquered' in the account of their experience. For Allier, it was a clear sense of the old 'I' having been overcome (p. 436). He concluded that to say that birth was preceded by death was less correct than to say that both experiences coincided or 'arrived at the same instant', and that this was true whether it was a case of gradual or sudden conversion. In both cases it is manifestly real because of the 'new orientation of deep emotions' and 'changes of tastes and aversions' (p. 531). As conversion is a redirection of the entire being there is no difference of essential nature between sudden and gradual conversions, though there may be differences of degree (pp. 548–9).

Even in those cases where conversion is a collective phenomenon, a scholar like Lévy-Bruhl had recognized that conversion is incomplete, unless it includes the conversion of the individual (p. 558). Like William James, Allier realized that the experience was authoritative to the individual: 'In the hour of conversion it presents itself as a dawning of the truth', while 'the ideas . . . acquire a new power of realization' (p. 525). We may close this treatment of Allier's work with his handling of the place of the mind and the will in the conversion of the individual:

> In the first place conversion is a phenomenon which bypasses the intellectual . . . it is neither an action of the will nor . . . of the intelligence . . . we have seen how it forms a new 'me'. Is not this the matter [of importance] – the transposition of values, the emotional and intellectual aspect of this transformation – are not these simply the necessary concomitants of the appearance of this new 'me'? The essence of conversion is neither an excess of tears nor adherence to a formula: is it not rebirth? (Allier 1925, p. 526)

It is often difficult to know whether one writer has influenced another, but before leaving Allier it is interesting to notice how close the analysis of conversion given by the English historian A. D. Nock in his study *Conversion: Old and New in Religion from Alexander the Great to Augustine of Hippo* of 1993 was to Allier's. In his preface and the first of his lectures given at Trinity College, Dublin and at Harvard, Nock wrote:

> As a manifestation both of group solidarity and emergent indivi-
> dualism, it is a sociological phenomenon of the first importance
> . . . impulses which lie below the level of consciousness and produ-
> cing a delicate interplay between this and the intellect. (Nock
> 1933, p. vii)

By conversion,

> we mean the reorientation of the soul of an individual, his deliber-
> ate turning from an earlier piety for another, a turning which
> implies a consciousness that a great change is involved, that the
> old way was wrong and the new is right.

Lewis Rambo

To read Lewis Rambo's study *Understanding Religious Conversion* of 1993 was to become aware of the intensive concentration of the social sciences and psychology on the phenomenon in the years since James and Allier wrote their accounts. Since 1980 alone, Rambo is able to point to some fifteen articles on conversion in learned journals of these disciplines and this apart from the large theological and missiological output. Rambo, who himself experi-enced conversion and admits himself to be on a voyage of self-discovery on the subject, like Allier before him, discovered in the field of mission studies a welcome resource for his work:

> Forays into cultural anthropology unveiled an existing discipline
> that provided new insights into the conversion process . . . subse-
> quently I discovered missiology, a field of scholarship initiated
> by missionaries working in cross-cultural settings that confront
> them daily with the complexities of interwoven religious,
> cultural and societal issues affecting and effecting change.
> (Rambo 1993, p. xi)

Rambo has regarded conversion as a radical experience in the precise sense of 'striking at the root of the human predicament', a root which he described as 'a vortex of vulnerability' (p. xii). He showed himself to share some of William James's pragmatism, when he wrote, 'Stated starkly, conversion is what a faith group says it is', though this definition, applied here to sectarian groups, can be inclusive presumably of the early Church's emphasis on conversion to Christ, with which this paper began. He appealed to A. D. Nock, who had also emphasized the radical nature of conversion in the prophetic religions of Judaism and Christianity and by contrast to pagan religion in the ancient world (pp. 5, 34–5).

Stages of Conversion

Rambo presents a seven-stage sequential model of conversion consisting of context, crisis, quest, encounter, interaction, commitment and consequences (p. 17). Missiologists have generally urged attention to context. Rambo holds that the context 'shapes the nature, structure and process of conversion' and that conversion takes place 'in a dynamic context' (p. 20). For Western Christianity this has sobering implications in Rambo's view. Religion is in decline and (following Berger) is relegated to the private realm, while a 'unified religious view seems less plausible' (p. 28). Rambo guesses that in such a context, parents will have more difficulty in retaining their children within the faith; and, further, that a declining religion will proselytize (his use of word) less (p. 34). Looking at non-Western societies he notices that certain social scientists see people as active agents of social change and he specifies missionaries as such agents (p. 56). He wrote: 'In many instances missionaries were rather remarkable people who fought for the welfare of the nations and sought to save them in an altruistic manner' (p. 69). In terms of conversions, so much depended on his view on

> the 'right' potential convert coming into contact, in the proper circumstances at the proper time, with the 'right' advocate and religious option. Trajections of potential converts and available advocates do not often meet in such a way that the process can germinate, take root and flourish. (Rambo 1993, p. 87).

Such an analysis is borne out by, for instance, the conversion of the Japanese leader, Kagawa, and the American missionaries who met him at his point of need (Axling 1932, pp. 1–17), as with many others. Relationships of this kind are central to conversion experiences for Rambo: he instances the personal influence of C. S. Lewis on Sheldon Vanauken, author of *A Severe Mercy*, or of the Christian industrialist Tom Phillips on Charles Colson as evidenced in Colson's *Born Again* (p. 135). Like both James and Allier, he identified the element of self-abandonment, whereby a confession of helplessness and an inability to care for the self (as, for example, in many participants in Alcoholics Anonymous) paradoxically begins the road back. Again, like the earlier writers, he discerns that energy is released, previously devoted to an inner conflict now resolved, and becomes 'available for new life'.

If we revert to our original threefold definition of Christian conversion, Rambo gives little on conversion to Christ, though he notes the case of Eldridge Cleaver, whose childhood image of Jesus re-emerged at his conversion 'as a symbol of healing and transformation' (pp. 25–6); perhaps this is assumed, as he moves in a Christian cultural context much as William James does. More seriously, he seems to ignore almost wholly the aspect of conversion to community, symbolized for Christians by baptism as both sign of new life and membership of Christ's Church. He might reply that, as I have omitted Allier's second volume, dealing with the consequences of conversion, he is entitled to isolate what Allier calls 'the crisis'. Nevertheless, in one who gives so much space to the social context of conversion, it is surprising that so little is given on the social and communal aspect of the convert.

When it comes to behaviour, however, Rambo does offer guidance: the convert has to move from irresponsible to responsible behaviour and this includes intellectual responsibility in the refutation of false ideology. Ethically, the convert learns to transcend personal gratification and begins to live for justice in an 'other-directed' fashion, so that his conversion can be described as socio-political (pp. 146–7, 202). Finally, he sees the test of conversion in whether it becomes an ongoing transformation:

> I would agree that people who convert and remain the same are not really on a path of transformation. They ... relive the event over and over again but it has little power to transform their lives. Change is persistent and important and continuing and most religious traditions expect and foster change by providing ideology and techniques for the ongoing development and maturation of their members. (Rambo 1993, p. 163)

Conclusion

What does this review of three studies of conversion tell us as students of mission? First, it gives evidence of the kind of inner tension involved for individuals personally addressed by the Christian message, what James calls 'the divided self' and Allier the 'two Is'. There is a deep and painful awareness of living in two contexts, of having 'two hearts', a situation too painful to continue without resolution. For example, the resort to relief on the part of Africans by way of galloping horses is an expression of the tension and pressure on the inner life.

Second, there is clear evidence of how much of this struggle goes on subliminally. The example of the man under the chloroform is particularly instructive. To say this is not to invite the Christian persuaders to adopt subliminal approaches, a method at odds with a proper respect for the human intellect and will; but it may lead, for example, to a reassessment by Western Christians of the place of dreams, for example, in conversion. A Judaeo-Christian tradition, which in its source documents contains decisive dreams in the Joseph saga and in the early spread of Christianity, as in the case of Paul at a turning point of his missionary activity (Genesis 37.2–11; 40.7–23; 41.1–37; Acts 16.9),[1] may have to be open, like the missionary Hermann Dieterlen, to the reassessment of the dream world; was William James right that the subliminal door may at times be the route by which external influence is brought to bear? Most primal settings in Africa and elsewhere sit more easily with the accounts of dreams in the Old and New Testaments than do modern Westerners.

Again, the radical nature of conversion in the loss of one identity and the development of a new one described by the writers in terms of death and life, should bring home the profound issues at stake in all Christian mission: to quote Stephen Neill:

> What is it that has died? It is I myself. It is the self which, in its pride, has organised itself in independence of God and in rebellion against him. And does it want to die? It clings to life with the fury of despair. It is prepared to go to any length, to make any kind of compromise with God, if only it may be let off dying. That is why it is so hard to be converted; that is why we must never lightly use the expression 'faith in Christ'. (Neill 1960, p. 41)

The same writer reminds us, in his call for a modern William James, that far from conversion being an adolescent phenomenon alone (a position William James also opposed), many well-known figures of the modern Christian world have been adult converts, including such intellectuals as Bulgakov, Berdyaev, Maritain, Marcel, T. S. Eliot, C. S. Lewis, the Cambridge classical teacher Martin Charlesworth, to whom A. D. Nock dedicated his work *Conversion*, and many others (Neill 1978, pp. 207–8).

Tension, subconscious struggles, discovery of a new identity by way of a form of dying: these factors underline the deeply radical nature of conversion as described by Rambo and the radical personal change which is at the heart of the Christian experience. It can well be asked: what is the justification for focusing on conversion in an international conference[2] devoted to a Christian critique of the world economy? Perhaps, however, there is a connection. For, in both cases, at the macro- and the micro-level, the Christian gospel calls for change. In Karl Barth's words on conversion, 'When we convert and are renewed in the totality of our being, in and with a private responsibility we also accept a public responsibility' (Barth 1969, p. 565). Like R. H. Tawney, the Christian economist at the Jerusalem conference of 1928, I do not believe that in order to change society you have to change the hearts of men first (Tawney 1928, pp. 164, 169; Yates 1994, pp. 68–9); but, in so far as the call to conversion is a call to action, as Lesslie Newbigin's definition suggested, to align a life with the new reality of the Kingdom of God and so with the divine will for justice and love, means individual lives so surrendered may indeed contribute, and contribute importantly, to a changed world order, towards that cosmic transformation which the Christian believes to be God's intention.

Notes

1 Loisy, Haenchen, Rachham and Lampe all consider Paul's 'vision' of the Macedonian 'during the night' to have been a dream.
2 This article is a revised version of a paper at the 9th International Congress of the International Association for Mission Studies in Buenos Aires 1996.

References and Further Reading

Allier, R. (1925), *La Psychologie de la conversion chez les peuples non-civilisés*, Paris: Payot. (Translation from the French is the writer's throughout.)

Axling, W. (1932), *Kagawa*, London: SCM Press.

Barth, K. (1969), *Church Dogmatics IV/2*, Edinburgh: T. and T. Clark.

Drabble, M. (ed.) (1985), *Oxford Companion to English Literature*, Oxford: Oxford University Press, entry 'Pragmatism'.

James, W. ([1902] 1977), *The Varieties of Religious Experience*, Glasgow: Collins.

Jones, E. S. (1960), *Conversion*, London: Hodder and Stoughton.

Kittel, G. (ed.) (1965), *Theological Dictionary of the New Testament* IV (tr. G. W. Bromley), Grand Rapids, MI: Eerdmans.

Neill, S. C. (1950), 'Conversion', *Scottish Journal of Theology*, 3 (4).

Neill, S. C. (1960), *What is Man?*, London: USCL.

Neill, S. C. (1978), 'Conversion', *Expository Times* 89 (7), pp. 205–8.

Newbigin, L. (1969), 'Conversion' in Neill, S., Anderson, G. H. *et al.* (eds), *Concise Dictionary of the Christian World Mission*, London: SCM Press.

Nock, A. D. (1933), *Conversion: The Old and the New in Religion from Alexander the Great to Augustine of Hippo*, Oxford: Clarendon Press.

Parker, T. H. L. (1982), 'Conversion' in Richardson, A., *A Dictionary of Christian Theology*, London: SCM Press.

Rambo, L. (1993), *Understanding Religious Conversion*, New Haven, CT: Yale University Press.

Tawney, R. H. in International Missionary Council (1928), *Report of the Jerusalem Meeting of the International Missionary Council* V, Jerusalem: IMC.

Yates, T. (1994), *Christian Mission in the Twentieth Century*, Cambridge: CUP.

INDEX

The Society for Promoting Christian Knowledge (SPCK) was founded in 1698. It has as its purpose three main tasks:

- **Communicating the Christian faith in its rich diversity**
- **Helping people to understand the Christian faith and to develop their personal faith**
- **Equipping Christians for mission and ministry**

SPCK Worldwide serves the Church through Christian literature and communication projects in over 100 countries. Special schemes also provide books for those training for ministry in many parts of the developing world. SPCK Worldwide's ministry involves Churches of many traditions. This worldwide service depends upon the generosity of others and all gifts are spent wholly on ministry programmes, without deductions.

SPCK Bookshops support the life of the Christian community by making available a full range of Christian literature and other resources, and by providing support to bookstalls and book agents throughout the UK. SPCK Bookshops' mail order department meets the needs of overseas customers and those unable to have access to local bookshops.

SPCK Publishing produces Christian books and resources, covering a wide range of inspirational, pastoral, practical and academic subjects. Authors are drawn from many different Christian traditions, and publications aim to meet the needs of a wide variety of readers in the UK and throughout the world.

The Society does not necessarily endorse the individual views contained in its publications, but hopes they stimulate readers to think about and further develop their Christian faith.

For further information about the Society, please write to:
SPCK, Holy Trinity Church, Marylebone Road,
London NW1 4DU, United Kingdom.
Telephone: 0171 387 5282